Tryst 2000:

The Falkirk Millennium Anthology

In Fond Memory

*Norman MacCaig, Iain Crichton Smith
and Nigel Tranter*

"Your licht burned aff the harr."

Tryst 2000:

The Falkirk Millennium Anthology

Editor Joy Hendry

Falkirk Writers Circle 2000

Falkirk Writers Circle
c/o Barbara Hammond
14 Ladysgate Court
Falkirk FK2 8HE
Scotland

The publisher acknowledges the financial assistance of
Awards for All Scotland and the Scottish Arts Council.

A catalogue record for this volume is
available from the British Library.
ISBN 0-9515699-4-5

Printed by
Inglis Allen
Middlefield Road, Falkirk FK2 9AG

Acknowledgements

In the making of this book, the members of Falkirk Writers' Circle would like to thank the Scottish Arts Council and the Awards for All Programme for recognising a worthy project and putting together the funding which made it all possible.

We would also like to acknowledge the technical expertise of Chapman Publishing and the help received from editor Joy Hendry. We would also like to thank the many established writers who have entertained us and give so freely of their time adjudicating our seminar and club competitions. But, before rattling through the full supporting cast, a special debt of gratitude must go to our long-suffering tutors, whose knowledge, experience and dedication has been the inspirational driving force behind so much of the Circle's work.

Tutors

Kath Hardie, Rennie McOwan, Jim McIntosh, Evelyn Hood, Pat Gerber, Sheila Lewis and Stephen Mulrine.

Adjudicators

Iain Crichton Smith, Stewart Conn, Joy Hendry, Sheila Lewis, Robin Lloyd-Jones, Geddes Thomson, Margaret Gillies Brown, Margaret Thomson Davies, Stephen Mulrine, Rennie McOwan, Sylvie Taylor, Ailie Scullion, Donald Campbell, Emil Pacholek, Joyce Begg, Robin Bell, Janet Paisley, Cathie MacPhail, Anna Blair, Maurice Lindsay, Duncan Glen, Margaret McKinlay, Eileen Ramsay, Ian Scott, Sheila Livingston, Mike Paterson, Marion McLean, Alanna Knight, Jim C Wilson and Kenneth C Steven.

Speakers

Norman MacCaig, Liz Lochhead, David Campbell, Mike Dition, Hugh Rae, Hugh Brown, Alan Wilding, Jean Blackwood, Rowena Goffin, Elizabeth Casciani, Fredrick Lindsay, Brian McCabe, Carl MacDougall, Margaret Ryan, Duncan Williamson, Ray Smith, Pam Williamson, Aileen Paterson and Nigel Tranter.

Cover photograph by Kevin Scott.

Contents

Dr Rennie McOwan

Introduction

Who would not want to see major diseases cured, poverty wiped out and war ended and we all hope for that in the years ahead? Within all that, there is another aspect of life which deserves attention, the life of the spirit.

Many people live lives of quiet desperation. Many people face crushing burdens and yet – so fittingly and appropriately our musicians still write tunes and sing songs and our writers still produce poems, books, articles and plays.

This life of the cultural spirit is desperately important for the common weal and our writers and musicians should be treated as special people and, as well as their work being examined critically, they should be given financial and other help to produce their offerings.

There is a famous quotation by James Elroy Flecker about a country not honouring poetry deserving to be castigated, disgraced and forgotten.

Drummond of Hawthornden wrote centuries ago: "Make an eternal spring. Give life to this dark world that lyeth dead". He wanted to see an outpouring of song, poetry, story, so that the spirit and the souls of people would be enriched.

Our new Scottish Parliament may not be as politically powerful as some of us would wish, but it was enlightening to see and hear that the formal opening ceremonies included three poems, one from a girl who was too shy to read it herself, one by our lamented and dear friend, the late Iain Crichton Smith, which spoke of Scotland's three languages and the need for friendship, and one by Robert Burns, his great anthem poem about social equality, so movingly sung by Sheena Wellington.

That promises so much. The tradition of the makars of Scottish literary history lives on and the many writers groups up and down the country continue that tradition, gatherings of like-minded people who want to make something, to create something, which will enlarge their happiness and their spirit and, hopefully, will do the same for other people.

Some people in writers' groups lack confidence. Some do not know where their strengths and weaknesses lie. Some have fallen through the education net in earlier years. Others have only found time in their later years to think and to write.

An immense amount of excellent poetry and fiction is produced by writers' groups and it is good that so much financial help has come from the local authorities, the Scottish Arts Council and the Scottish Book Trust. The standard of this anthology, for example, is very high.

People like myself who have been tutors to writers' groups or worked with school pupils or students in creative writing projects know the worth of what is produced and what is lying there untapped.

I would like to see more financial help being given so that groups can enlarge their activities. I would like to see new and more national awards for writers and a new strand of Scottish literary honours created whereby writers of talent were given greater bursaries and, where applicable, pensions and awards equal to or greater than the current honours like OBEs and MBEs. I would like to see more financial help for Scottish publishing firms and less London parochialism in the broadcasting field because a country that does not help its own cannot be truly international in outlook.

Every congratulation to the writers whose work appears in this anthology, to the new makars of today. Every best wish to the makars of the future, some of whom will read this volume.

Lord Ewing of Kirkford

Winston Churchill, when a very sick old man, ended his penultimate speech in the House of Commons with these words;

> The day may dawn when fair play, love for one's fellow man, respect for justice and freedom, will enable tormented generations to march forth, serene and triumphant, from the hideous epoch in which we dwell. Meanwhile, never flinch, never weary and never despair.

That comment was made nearly fifty years ago yet somehow as we march forth into this new millennium the sentiments in total, and the detail in part, are as relevant now as they were when Churchill spoke those words.

Where then do I look for the greatest hope held out by the advent of the new millennium?

It is tempting indeed to produce a shopping list of hopes for the future but I propose to resist that temptation and concentrate on one great hope which, I know millions of people will share with me.

In recognising that the last millennium in general, and the final century of that millennium in particular, produced absolutely bewildering advances in the field of medicine, discovering cures for illness that hitherto had been incurable, I recognise also that, despite the outstanding efforts of all who work in the field of medical science and research, a cure for cancer has so far eluded us.

One thing I am totally certain of in the new millennium and that is that people are going to live much longer than ever before.

Accepting that as I do, the quality of that long life becomes absolutely crucial and this leads me to my overriding hope for the new millennium that sooner rather than later, first of all a cure will be found for cancer and followed quickly by a treatment that will prevent this dreaded condition in the first place.

Dennis Canavan

Revolutionary Ideas for a New Millennium

The new millennium will present many challenges and great opportunities and here are three of my wishes for a better future.

My first wish is for the success of the Millennium Canal Link. The hub of the project will be here in Falkirk, where the two canals will be reunited by the magnificent Millennium Wheel, a unique and marvellous feat of modern engineering which will continue to be a symbol of the Millennium long after the Greenwich Dome has been forgotten. Falkirk was the birthplace of the Industrial Revolution. The Wheel at Tamfourhill will also be revolutionary in more ways than one. The Millennium Link has the potential to regenerate the local economy and improve the environment of Central Scotland.

The Wheel could attract visitors from all over the world and we must seize that opportunity to show them other aspects of our local heritage. The Antonine Wall and Rough Castle are of great historical interest. The two Battles of Falkirk are important landmarks in Scottish history and we should not forget the courage of those who gave their lives in the working class rebellion at the Battle of Bonnymuir. For those interested in architecture and the environment, Callendar House and the surrounding Park could be major attractions. The Millennium Link is the most exciting thing to happen in Falkirk for many years and, if the people of Falkirk rise to the occasion, then it could herald a new era of opportunity for the entire community.

My second wish is for an improvement in educational opportunities for all, but especially for our young people. In recent years we have seen the clock being turned back with the abolition of student grants and the introduction of loans and tuition fees. The Scottish Executive's response to the Cubie Report is hopelessly inadequate and, as we enter a new millennium, ministers must be made to realise that investment in education is an investment in our future.

My third and most important wish is that the new millennium will bring a peaceful revolution leading to a new world order. The millennium which has just finished surely taught us many lessons about the futility of war. The last century alone saw two World Wars, the first of which was supposed to be the war to end all wars but clearly it did no such thing. It was followed by the Holocaust and the use of weapons of mass destruction which still threaten the very existence of the human race. At the same time, innocent children are dying daily because of poverty, disease and malnutrition in developing countries.

If we all work harder for peace and justice throughout the world, we shall help to ensure that the new millennium will mean a new beginning and a better future for the bairns of the Third World as well as the bairns of Falkirk.

Evelyn Hood

Why Write?

Why? That's what my family always wanted to know as I grew up, veering giddily between reading everything I could get my hands on and scribbling on the back of every abandoned envelope when nothing better was within reach. Why do you keep wanting to write, they asked plaintively? That's what I want to know too, but so far, many years, many rejections and many publications later, I still don't have the answer – 'How long is a piece of string?' – 'Who and what is God?'

Writing is like the north face of the Eiger. Mountaineers climb the Eiger because it is there and writers write because that is what they do. It's a challenge, it's fun, it's hell, it' s a reason for living, and it keeps us off the streets. Well, some of us, anyway.

It is an itch that can't be removed by scratching. I hate it because it gets in the way of my social life and I love it because I know that no matter how old and wise I may become, no matter how much I may write, I will never master the craft. There will always be something new to learn: a different, better, more exciting storyline than I have ever thought up before may be waiting just around the corner. And isn't that a wonderful prospect?

Before the written word, there were the bards, minstrels and story-tellers, men and women who travelled the land from community to community telling stories in song, poetry and prose. When man learned to read and write those tellers of tales, often based on living history, were able to reach a wider audience.

People have always loved learning of their past and their world by stories, songs, poems and plays. The ability to listen and read and learn from the spoken and written word is a bonus, and the ability to communicate by both is a precious gift indeed.

Even in this high-technology world, on the first step of a new millennium, the spinners of tales, the songsters, the poets and playwrights have their place. And, for the sake of humanity, may that always be so.

Alex Totten

My Thoughts for the Millennium

Looking forward to the new millennium is, for me, like looking towards the next game. Inevitably it means looking back and being aware of the things that have gone before, trying to learn from mistakes and making sure they are not repeated. As manager of Falkirk Football Club I am acutely aware that I am merely the current custodian of that position and that the club is now entering its third century. In its time the football club has acted as a focus for the community and even in recent times it has shown the best of the traditional values of community spirit and mutual support.

Just a few years ago the club reached the final of the Scottish Cup Competition and it was marvellous to be part of the occasion and the sense of identity it gave Falkirk. This small achievement seemed to bring out the best in the community, and everyone in the town was proud to be associated with the team. Then when the club were in dire financial straits again the community, including the supporters we seldom see, were there with their tangible support and their determination not to let part of Falkirk's history disappear. It is in times of celebration and times of adversity that Falkirk people pull together.

These examples of what could be achieved when we all pull together and support each other is almost a reflection of a football team. In a team each player has his own level of skill and ability but, without the support and complimentary talents of his team mates, very little of consequence can be achieved. It is when the team plays as a team, with each member contributing to the best of their ability, that seemingly impossible goals are achieved. As was evidenced when we defeated Celtic over two games to reach the Scottish Cup Final.

There have been so many advances over the last century, with positive benefits for society but at a cost. At present we live in a society that appears to have lost its sense of community, where everyone is out to get what they want with little regard for others – and the poorer we are for that. We undervalue the contribution other members of our community team can make, particularly those we regard as less able, and yet there are so many examples where the whole is much greater than the sum of its parts.

On the positive side, everyone has the opportunity to achieve all they can, but we must also be responsible for ensuring that we protect those less fortunate than ourselves and respect their talents and abilities to be used in our community team.

Football is a very traditional sport and is rightly termed the people's game. Sometimes it assumes too prominent a position in our daily life when there are more important issues to be considered but as a focus for our community and wider, our nation, it still his a role to play. My main hope for the future would be that many of the values that can take a football club to the top, such as mutual respect for others, appreciation of many and varied talents, hard work and dedication and the need to work together, should be reflected once more in our community.

I hope we can regain some of the traditional values that we seem to have lost and begin to have more respect for others and, in doing so, have more respect for ourselves. We can do it, we have done it before, but, rather than just in times of celebration or times of adversity, why don't we try to do it every day?

Jordan Alma

Do You Understand Me?

When I say that I understand you
what I mean is that I'm able
to stand under you.
In your shoes, sometimes in your slippers,
even in your bare feet.
Do you understand me?
Can you stand under me?
Never in my shoes, never in my slippers.
You're always under my feet.

The Grieving Clock

Tick, tock, tick, tock.
Is anyone listening
to the tick, tock, tick, tock?
My hands move round my face
to another hour, another day.
No one looks at me any more.

I miss your presence, your watchful gaze.
I kept you in order!
Time to get up, time to go to work
I made sure you got there on time.
Four o'clock, you knew you needed to rest,
six o'clock, I told you to eat,
ten o'clock, I called you to bed.
Am I redundant now?

Tick, tock, tick, tock.
Three weeks on. Will you come back?
I have no purpose any longer,
no duty to perform. My existence in question?
But I tick, therefore I am!

I hang on the wall – a mere ornament
without admirers.
Tick, tock, tick, tock,
in the ominous silence.
I echo in the empty space.
I miss my master. When will you return?
Who will replace my batteries?
I fear my time is running out.
I fear my long life is coming to an end.
But I am loyal, I will work for you.
I am hopeful, I will wait for you.

I will go through the motions
of tick, tock, tick, tock,
longing for your return,
awaiting attention:
your warm and loving smile,
your love of life.
I am the structure to your days.
I am time.
Time waits for you.

Hugh Bateman

Mother

I've had my three score years and ten
Certainly won't return again
Still I hear my mother's cry
Perhaps my poem may tell you why

Still summer eve walking slowly by
I hear a window open heard a mother cry
Twas then this heartfelt anguish
Before was full of glee as a childish heart first
told me no mother's call for me

Yet somewhere in heart's chamber
There echoes in the mind
This precious voice kept saying
Bairnie never mind
Patience patience loved one
I only lie asleep
But as our blessed Saviour
What I have I keep

So don't look downward dear one
At this well trodden sod
Just let your soul fly upwards
And greet the face of God

For you're not the only orphan
To bear this heavy load
There's many loved kin before you
To brighten your abode

Lorna Binnie

The Water Bearer

My Gemini twins have now left to fulfil their ambitions and destiny. Looking back, there was Pop, Hippies, Punk, then nappies. My growing children burst balloons whilst eating junk food. Anxious days and nights.

Alone, in my candle-lit Feng-Shui room awaiting the dawn of the age of Aquarius.

The Deserted Hospital

A single shoe lies in the shadow of the sun,
amidst the uncut summer grass, slowly waltzing, in the breeze.
silently stretching its roots, swirling in tempo
turning quick to golden hay.

Nearby the rusty drainpipe creaks,
Home to chirpy sparrows that nested in Spring.
Now never disturbed by the hand of the painter
that longed to renew its grey.

No elderly people crossing the zebra lines
gripping firmly their steel capped sticks.
Old council signs for wards 7, 8 and 9 stand erect
where worn eyes would watch for drivers driving slowly.

Shell-like buildings belonging to the 2nd World War era
whose torn curtains wander against the vandalised windows.
Their walls echo whispering voices from forgotten memories
and faint laughter from joyous times past.

A chair overturned perches unconfined
next to the wild sweet lotion balm rose garden,
yearning for Grandma to straighten it and bolster its ragged
     cushion
No ghosts live here.

Only the exit of weary bodies and confused minds.
Spirits of the post-war good life that have departed
and sit in some other place.

Letter for the Millennium
from Anne Hathaway

Ye Friends and Writers of the Future,

Today I have instructed my Stratford attorney to release this letter and its secrets to you Falkirk Writers in the Year of our Lord 2000. It has been held in safe keeping and stored through generations of attorneys who, I hope, will deliver it unopened to ye.

It is early summer as I sit by my window looking out across my sweet-smelling apple-blossomed garden. I have herbs in abundance that flavour my food and scent my clothes on warm days.

Sad! No not I, but happy the old bugger is dead. Do you know who I mean? Olde Bill, well, his real name is William Shakespeare. His last will and testament was read today, but I was not shocked by its content. My small bequest, by this lecherous man, husband and father of my children, was: "I give unto my wife my second best bed and furniture."

You see the best bed was secretly sent off to London with a letter, two cheeses and 10 shillings to his mistress Viola the day after William died. To be fair, he left everything to Susanna, my beloved daughter, now married to Doctor Hall, an eminent physician – the small girl who Will held in his lap and teased, calling her 'Greensleeves' when she could not find a cloth for her nose.

The other reason for sleeping in the second best bed was his bad breath. He was obsessed by it. You can read about his obsessions with it in his work, if they have survived the ages. In *A Midsummer Night's Dream* Bottom warns "Eat neither onions or garlic for we are to utter sweet breath". While in the *Henry the VI* play a character says: "His breath stinks like eating toasted cheese". In *Julius Caesar* there is a reference to the stinking breath of the crowd. However in *The Taming of the Shrew* one character is found to perfume the air.

I myself often sucked on cloves whilst in his company and filled my hair with rose water, especially latterly to make his last days smelling of heaven on earth.

Our private life was short and probably never documented until now. You may think that he married me for my money, a woman more than seven years his senior. Well, that was true. Will would have done anything for a quill. Yet there was a passion, The first day I saw him he was hanging around the Guildhall, watching the travelling players. It was Whitsun, the day was warm and he was standing beside Ye Olde Oak Tree, with hand on hip, drinking wine and ginger and slightly intoxicated. It was not his looks that caught me but what he said with loud melody:

> Shall I compare thee to a summer's day,
> Thou art more lovely and more temperate,
> Rough winds do shake the darling buds of May,
> And summer's lease hath all too short a date

Nobody had spoken to me like that before. I was impressed, a farmer's daughter who had endured cows and cow dung for company. His tender words imprinted a longing for his body and soul. It was not long until we were married. I had a small dowry and could not hope for a better match. He made me feel good, happy to love all things alive. The money would not last forever and I hoped that Will would love me but I soon realised that he loved another. Not a person but a desire to write and act.

Stratford was not the place to secure patronage; he had to go to London. Will had a brilliance and I would not be the one to stop him. He loved London and made a number of financially advantageous arrangements, and had shares in the Globe and Blackfriars theatres. He even gave special presentations to Queen Elizabeth, who it was said had a special liking for him.

I would write to him often and ask,

> O William, William, wherefore art though William? Deny thy father and refuse thy name, or if thou will not be sworn, my love, and I'll no longer be a Shakespeare.

He did not reply, that is not until just before he returned home, eight years before he died. I know Will had queens, ladies and whores. He had such a passionate intensity about him and like a master of emotion he had to experience the deepest levels of human motivation to enable him to write the way he did.

For ye writers of Falkirk in the year of our Lord 2000 I leave behind a memory, a sonnet, of the life of a great man. A woman who has loved and despised, and ignored and cared for a man who has penned the vast land between heaven and earth.

> Nor tears, nor prayers shall purchase and abuse,
> Therefore have none, remember him,
> The runaways eyes may wink, and William,
> Leap to the arms, untalked of and unseen,
> Far away in land, in no civil night,
> Come home, love family by day doth night,
> Or shut those eyes and resign the quill,
> Spread the close curtain, love performing knight.

Behind every successful man lies a woman, waiting.

Your sincere friend,

Anne Hathaway, Stratford-upon-Avon, May 23rd 1616

Allan Brownlie

Sweet, Sweet Countess

Dear Countess,
Do you remember one morning you walked to my cottage
and drank the milk, warm from the cow's udder?
Do you remember when I led your droves to Falkirk
and how you delighted in tales of the raids,
mythical or not?

But now we have grown so far apart –
as hate is from love;
further apart than even death itself.
Our languages are incomprehensible.
I do not understand your sherry cabinets –
or you my Gaelic verbs.

It is all exile now that the severance has come;
be it Canada, Glasgow, or Uist.

You have taken me from all that was mine
and given me wine, bitter with gall.

You told me I was the cause of my own misfortune
by foolishly losing at Culloden,
by bringing children and poverty to the glen
so that only mass eviction remained
as the solution for you in your glass castle –
a regrettable hindrance to your plan
and a pang for your conscience.

If brochures were available
I would have received the glossy ones,
advertising the corn prairies of Canada
and the promised land of Govan.
They opened their doors to heroes
made useless by certification of clanship and trust,
heroes who died for their land and chieftain
even when they knew that betrayal hung in the air.

You told me that, in the circumstances,
exile was the best solution
and that Canada offered great prospects
for a man like me,

who could sing our poetry in Toronto and Montreal
and travel on those great lakes,
free from the crippling poverty of the glens
and the battles that destroyed my friends.

You almost convinced me
that even Glasgow,
was an appropriate environment
for an alcoholic poet to become a phoenix,
– if only a Highland phoenix.

The certificate came through the door today,
requiring just a signature of acceptance.
Strathnaver and Kildonan and Dachau
and Warsaw and Prague stare back at me.
I have the pen again in my raised hand
to sign on the dotted line of the lesser evil.

At least you are honest in your hatred,
clearing the glens of the untidy remnants
of your people
so that not a hearth or stone or surname
will remain to haunt you
with the human cry of your folly.

And you do not understand
that I cannot just rise and go
with a song in my heart
and my bunnet in the air,
like a well-paid extra in *Brigadoon* by the sea.

Sweet Countess,
ask me why I want to remain
in this poverty-stricken glen
with nothing but the bare hills
and my dun cow?

Can you not understand
that I do not want your gowns
or your castle,
your Aryan perfection
or the gold mines that split the Transvaal?

Understand
that you do not want my bread
and my warm milk,

my poetic uncertainty
or the dances that make an Autumn worthwhile?

Is it possible for either of us to understand
that what I want are the bare Highland stones
and those blades of grass I crushed
with my bare feet
as I walked from Culloden for you
into the burning glens.
I want the sounds we made as we danced in Edinburgh
and the river and the trees
and the byre and the sky,
and anything that would reassure us
that everything is not an eternal void
for me and you –,

Sweet, sweet Countess.

Laverock

Oh laverock, sae near my window singin,
sing na, oh sing na here,
but eident tae the hills gae wingin
an greet my dear.

An tell her, in the sang you're liltin,
on her I dwine,
like gress that on the field lies wiltin
in the het hairst time.

When she's no by me, heich in the lift the mune
for me rides dim;
an there's sma solace in the simmer sun,
nae warmth in him.

Tell her that canty sang and jest
she's taen awa,
an I can find nae bield tae rest,
nae bield ava.

Oh laverock, sae near my window singin,
sing na, oh sing na here,
but eident tae the hills gae wingin
an greet my dear.

Andrew Burnside

Winter Journey

Brown and straw and green
The winter fields run by
The speeding train;
Brown and grey and black
The winter bark of trees,
The cuttings and their stone.

Blue and cold and clear
Without a trace of cloud
The winter day;
Low and pale and sharp
Upon the passing eye
The winter sun.

Old and long familiar
This winter journey,
This last, this century;
Fresh and bright and new
This railway journey,
This winter journey.

Minnows

You always had to queue up for a boat,
As "Number Ten!" blared out from the tannoy;
Across the pond, as far as he could get,
There he was – on *your* boat – some mutinous boy.

Apart from rowing, there wasn't much to
Do on a small, square, shallow, muddy, pond.
If only there had been an island or two –
To go exploring or row all round.

Instead, you'd trawl for minnows; with a jar
And a length of string, you'd terrorise fish;
So engrossing it was, you could be sure
To give *your* "Number Ten!" the complete miss!

Minnows, as far as I know, swim there still;
But of small boys and boats, the number's nil.

Stephen Cole

Meeting Strange Strangers

You are not running away?
No, I prefer to stay.
You are not afraid of the light?
All illumination is welcome in this miserable night.
This is the courage of desperation that answers us coldly.
I am author of the Holograph, I come and go boldly.
Yes, we know. We have inspected and selected: we know.
You know? How so?
We are the *Imago.*

What is your purpose, your business in this place?
To instruct and advise you on the progress of your race.
What must be said of Man's modern condition?
Uncertainty-transmitted equals dis-information –
And the mischievous aerial agency?
Refer back to earth all electrical contingency.

You are not flying away?
We are close to break of day.
You are not afraid of the sun?
We are leaving. Our task is done.
Now go now, all space/time unsizing
Go now, all fools talk despising
Go now, all feeling revising
We name you thus: *Imago Rising.*

Evelyn Conlan

Louis the Lip

He is smart and he is slick,
Sharp of tongue and sharp of wit,
Louis the Lip as he is known
People all hear when he comes to town.

At the gambling table he plays it cool,
Eyes like beacons darting here and there
His mind like the cards, sharp at the edge,
Played with precision, never loses a trick.

The others at the table, biting lips, scratching heads.
How can they compete with this unscrupulous little man?
Louis the Lip quietly piling up his spoils,
Smiling benignly at the other, shaking at the knees.

Gathering up his winnings, pockets bulging at the seams,
Performance over for this evening.
He straightens his tie, sleeks back his hair
Exit Louis the Lip.

Sharon Crozier

Smiling

Smiling is infectious
You can catch it like the flu.
Someone smiled at me today
And I started smiling too.

I passed around the corner
and someone saw the grin
When he smiled I realised
I'd passed it on to him!

I thought about the smile
And realised its worth,
A single smile like mine
Could travel round the earth.

So if you feel a smile begin
Don't leave it undetected.
Let's start an epidemic
And get the world infected.

Jean Currie

The Rations

"Will you go and get these messages?" said my mother as she shook the suds from her hands. She was a very pernickety woman and always seemed to have her hands in the suds. I wasn't so keen on soapy water and was often glad of an excuse to get out of washing the dishes, although I preferred washing to drying. When my brother and I had to share doing the dishes he always pushed me aside and washed, which meant I had to dry, but I usually got my own back by popping every second dish back in the basin and saying "dirty", which meant he had to wash them twice.

I grabbed the leather shopping bag, made sure the purse and ration books were inside, and went down the outside stair.

"Where are ye gaun, Jean?" called a well-known voice behind me. "Ah'll git ye up the road. Ah'm gaun fur the tatties." Tommy was really my brother's pal, a couple of years older than me, and some of the boys called him a 'Jessie' as he was always wanting to play at 'hooses' with me. Since there wasn't a girl of my age in the building and his mother made good chips I was happy at that naive age to have him as my pal. His house was downstairs from ours and I think he must have listened for my footsteps as he seemed to shadow me everywhere.

I knew he would be going to the Co-op for potatoes. His family were rationed there because you didn't pay till the end of the month, and he boasted they used half a stone of potatoes every day. So on Saturdays he had to struggle with a whole 14 pounds. We, on the other hand, were rationed with Stevenson the Grocer. I loved watching the owner take the butter-spades, dig into the barrel-shaped mass [fresh or salted] and expertly remove our allowance of ten ounces exactly, pat it from side to side, splashing drops of milky-looking liquid around, slip it onto a diminutive piece of greaseproof paper which barely covered it and slide it over the counter towards me. This slick manoeuvre always gave me the urge to be a grocer when I grew up. Then Mr Stevenson would take a pencil, a wartime one without paint, from behind his ear and mark a cross on the appropriate pages of each of our five ration books. These were legal documents, and we were warned that if they were damaged or destroyed they might not be replaced.

"Wait at Stevenson's and Ah'll get you doon the road," shouted

Tommy as he proceeded further up the hill to the Co-op. This annoyed me as they had to wait ages to be served in the 'Co', despite an elaborate system where you popped your book with your 'Co' number in a box and were served in rotation. My mother had warned me she wanted the messages for the tea quickly in a tone that meant she was in a bad mood. PMT was never mentioned in those days, but you had an instinct that on some days you obeyed without question.

"Ah've a new trick to show you," he called after me as I entered Stevenson's shop.

Eventually he arrived with his big open basket full of potatoes. I would like to have had a basket like that, but my mother said when the unwrapped bread was put on top of the other messages our kind of zipped bag kept the flies out.

"See this?" said Tommy as we walked along. He began to show off by circling his heavy basket round and round, faster and faster, sideways, up and down, diagonally, his body writhing in the same direction, his knitted tie flying out at right angles following his matching hand-knitted navy-blue jumper.

Off and on the pavement he ran, and miracle of miracles, not one tattie fell out. His face was crimson with effort and triumph by the time he stopped and blurted out,

"You try it noo."

"Naw, Ah'm feart," I replied as I hurried down the road,

"There's nuthin to be feart fur," coaxed Tommy, "You've got a zip on yer bag. But try it wi ma basket first."

Tentatively at first, but getting more and more courageous as not a tattie fell out, I felt absolutely elated at this magic.

"See, there's nuthin tae be feart fur," repeated Tommy, as he took back his basket and the two of us, yards apart, swung our basket and bag respectively round and round all the way home.

"See you the morn," shouted Tommy as he descended to his house and I climbed the stairs.

"You've been awfy long," grumped my mother as she took the bag. "Did Mr Stevenson have his eggs in?"

"Ay Mammy. Ah told him ma big brother was coming home on a 48 hour pass, and, do you know this? He gave me an extra egg. And Mammy, I can do a new trick."

My delight was short-lived as my mother began to unzip the shopping bag. Her face became crimson and at first she was speechless as her spotless fingers became soaked in a mixture of raw eggs, shells, ration books, big pennies, wee thrupennies and our precious ten ounces of butter.

That night I was sent to bed with a sore bottom and without

tea and dared to play with that Tommy Simpson again, but all was forgiven the next day when I went for the messages and Mr Stevenson slipped a jar of jam from under the counter into my pristine leather bag for my big brother 'off the ration'.

Grannie Gasbag

Ah'll always mind ma grannie, her sayins quite provocative,
But thinkin back on things she said, Ah'd say that she was
    talkative!

When Ah wis bit a lassie, an needin some advice,
She always had a sayin with a meaning so precise.

She'd criticise my cronie with "Her eggs have aye twa yolks"
Or if she didnae trust her, "She's mair faces than toon clockes".

Of friends of whom she disapproved, to give them up, I ought.
She'd say "If wi the craws ye flee, then wi the craws ye're shot."

If jealousy I sometimes felt of lovely Cousin Jane
"It's ithers jeely pieces that taste better than yer ain."

I'd often fly too high and then fall humbly in a heap,
She took delight in scolding, "That's your gas put at a peep."

Again I'd rise above myself, high-living I would feign.
She'd shak her heid and mutter, "Crofts an castles baith git rain."

"Mony a mickle maks a muckle" to make me save, she said,
And "Money's like the gairden dung, nae guid until it's spread."

If sometimes I was lazy, she'd hand me pots and pans.
"The deil will always find," said she, "some work for idle hands!"

When once a fly went in my ear when walking in the meadow,
Says Doctor Gran, "Now poke yer ear wi nothing but yer elbow."

"Taks twa tae fecht" an "Dinnae fash" "The ba's up oan the slates"
– These sayings all came pouring out, amusing all my mates.

I loved Wee Grannie dearly, and I never saw her sulk,
She certainly was tiny, but "Guid gear comes in sma bulk".

"The langest day will have an end," said grannie with a grin,
"My Maker's got me on his list, at death our lives begin."

I'm sure you're no surprised to learn ma grannie's now deceased,
I think I hear the Good Lord shout, "Oh grannie, *haud yer wheesht.*

Mary Duncan

Festival

They call her "Auld Reekie" but not for to-day.
To-day the city is in festive garb.
Gaily she swishes her skirts and shows her frilled petticoat.
Streets bedecked; lampposts garlanded; pennants aflutter.
We wait among the laughing crowds in the August sun.

Just out of sight, we hear the sound of the pipes.
Kilted bands from many countries march in proud procession.
Nearer and nearer they come. The excitement mounts.
We cannot talk. you would not hear;
we cheer instead, like tourists,

Flower-covered floats glide past:
dancers, jugglers, acrobats;
American marines marching and playing foot-tapping rhythm,
Canadian Mounties followed by exotic dancers
from some South Sea isle
Brilliant flamenco dancers flick castanets with stylish arrogance.
One tall silver-clad figure on stilts walks ten feet tall
the full length of Princes Street.

I lift my eyes to the splendour of the towering skyline.
Then lower my gaze; I try to capture it before it fades;
Mardi Gras has come to Edinburgh.

Nightfall, the theatre spills us out into darkness.
Music of the orchestra lingers in my head as I walk the streets.
Suddenly, a hand clutches my arm;
an old woman, bent and malodorous with drink and vomit;
a man calls to her from a darkened close.

Around a corner a young lad lies sleeping in a shop doorway,
curled up in foetal position.
An ambulance speeds by with urgent siren
and whirling blue light.
Night has come to the festival city.

Agnes Ford

At Last . . . I Think I've Got It!

Are you methodical? Organised? Efficient? Do you make shopping lists? Do you perhaps lay the tea table as soon as you've cleared the lunch things away?

Maybe I'm envious. Maybe I'd like to be more efficient. I tell myself that I'm perfectly happy trundling along life's highway in my disorganised 'muddle through somehow' manner.

Most of my friends are much more organised than I am. One particular friend always manages to produce, from the depths of her handbag, the exact thing you require at the precise moment you are in need of it. Such as a needle and thread to match the button that has thoughtlessly dislodged itself from your coat, or a rubber to wipe clean the price from a birthday card you just have to post right there and then. A headache powder. A sticking plaster . . . anything from an eartrumpet to a compass.

Sometimes against my better judgement I take advice from well-meaning efficient friends when I let slip that I've forgotten some item from the supermarket. "You should make a list," they tell me. But do I remember to put everything on my list?

And when I do make one I find myself wishing I'd taken the sideboard along to the shops, because that's where the list is; and what if I do find on my return there are two full jars of coffee in the cupboard and that the tea caddy is empty. And it was washing-up liquid I was out of and not washing powder. I'll get it right one day . . . maybe!

Walking in the country recently, my friend of 'the handbag' came to my rescue when my shoelace snapped with a piece of string she just happened to have in her pocket. She wasn't carrying 'the bag' and it set me wondering what else she might have secreted about her person. Should I feign a headache? Pretend to cut a finger? She couldn't be carrying all of life's necessities in her pocket.

Though grateful for the piece of string, I couldn't help feeling that my Girl Guide training had failed miserably. I just never seemed to be prepared! Or so I thought, until a few weeks ago when spending some time with the same friend in a holiday chalet up north.

"Take a hot water bottle," she had advised me. "It can be quite cold at nights."

Remembering that my one and only hot water bottle had leaked when last I'd used it, I paid my local ironmonger a visit.

"Do you have a stopper like this one?" I enquired. "You don't need a stopper, lass," he told me. "It's a new washer you want."

He produced a little packet labelled 'Hot Water Bottle Washers' containing four small rubber rings and obligingly fitted one to my stopper, assuring me, "That should do the trick."

I popped the three spares into my handbag and forgot about them, that is until the first night in our holiday chalet when we were preparing for bed. My friend despairingly announced that her hot water bottle was leaking.

Quick as a flash I told her, "It probably only needs a new washer."

"That's great," she said, with more than a trace of sarcasm. "And where do we find a washer at this time of night?"

I was already groping in my handbag. "Abracadabra – allow me." I fitted the new washer then turned the bottle upside down to demonstrate my handy work. "Look, not a drop."

"Where did you . . .? When did you . . . ?" my friend stuttered.

"Oh, I never go anywhere without spare hot water bottle washers," I lied. "You just never know when you might need one."

My moment of triumph had arrived. I'd scored at last!

Private Kwaku Forku's First Night on Guard Duty

"Halt – who be dat?"
"Dat be me."
"Who be dat say
'dat be me'
when I say
who be dat?

You be my friend
or you be foe?
Cos if you be foe
you go for go."

"I be your friend.
What be dis foe
you go for send?
I be your friend
and dat be me say
'dat be me'
when you say
'who be dat' ."

William Gray

Empty

Empty as hunger's plate
Licked clean
In barns of silent grain
Too weak to move or pose
With sucked out bones
And swollen bellies
That stare at cameras
Beamed wide on TV.

Sights that shock
Not once, not twice
But again and again.
Until too soon forgotten
Faded as a holiday tan
Hardened are the hearts
Towards two thirds of man.

Hotdogs in Brine

Balanced on driftwood
The boy declared himself a pirate
To fight for all the seashells
Uncovered by the closing tide.

Claiming right of possession
As far as the hotdog stand
Only screams of hungry seagulls
Dared swoop down in dispute.

Barking orders to a four-legged crew
To weigh anchor and set sail
He braced stern hands on hips
Till waves rolled over deck and shoes.

Salt water washed away the shine
Of seashells and dry socks
Now their rations were at a low
Still the hotdog stand was open.

Tattie Howkin

Early mornin, an jump oot ma bed, intae ma claes, an buits. Gien ma face a quick slunge in the cauld water, a dinnae feel sae sleepy noo. Efter a mouthfae o tea, A hurry tae meet the ither folk, at the fit o the street. We stand chattin, in the cauld dark, waitin fur the tractor tae come. "A bet ye he's slept in," moans a wumman tae hur neebour. A go ower an hae a laff wie Wullie, wha's in ma cless at the scule.

A kin hear the tractor comin a mile awa, oan this frosty mornin. We aw jump oan tae the trailer, while big Jock the fermer takes sum stick fur bein late. He disnae bother. He kens thir guid workers. A dinnae take up much room, bit A still get squashed, wi the big wumman sittin nixt tae me. At least she's keepin me warm, as A haud ma piece bag fur protection. "Ur yi aw right son?" she keeps askin, as the tractor an trailer go ower every bump on the road. It's great fun tho, like sittin in a bus withoot windaes, and yi kin see mair.

At last we're at the ferm – A could hiv walked here faster. A look ower the field at aw the tattie plants, thir's thoosants o thum. Still, A'm rairin tae go, it's better thin stannin aboot, bored and cauld. A've got ma ane stint – fur the first time A'll get twa pounds a day, fur daen it. It'll come in handy, fur ma mither is expectin again.

Big Jock mishers oot the stints wi big strides, poakin branches in the hard grund fur markers. Then he mairches back tae his tractor, an ploo, tae unearth the pink tatties. A stand dreamin fur a meenit, gazin at the huge sun, sittin like an orange oan the horizon. Lookin along the row, everybodie's started, an A mind whit wey A'm here.

A start luftin the tatties up, like thir pound notes, and throw thum intae ma wire basket. Ma fingers sting in the cauld earth, but A nivir raise ma heid till A've cleared row efter row. Sum folks start tae moan, "The fermer's goan too fast." But A'm feelin better noo A've warmed up.

It's tea time. We aw plod along tae the barn, tae sit oan dry bales o straw, bletherin an laffin. Hungry as usual, A eat aw ma pieces.

"How's yir ma keepin, Billy?"

"She's fine, Misses Mason," A reply.

"That's guid. Yi kin tell ur A'm askin fur hur."

"Wid yi like a piece, son?"

"Yes please, A'll keep it fur efter." We stert again, an afore long it's dinner time. A go fur a walk and clap the ferm collie, efter it's went roond mi a few times.

Finishin at fower – we're aw wearie, and wait fur the magic word fae Jock: "Right everybody, yis kin take sum tatties hame." A fill an auld hemp sack, luftin an layin it, A think this bag's heavier thun me, an A'm tired. Big Jock smiles, "Here's yir money, lad", handin me a broon envelope wi ma name writtin oan it. "A'll see yi the morn". Suddenly A feel great, an luft the bag o tatties nae bother ower tae the trailer, wi a big smile. Aw the road hame we sing an cairyoan, throwing tatties at telegraph poles – an onythin else that moves or disnae.

When A git hame, A say cheerio tae aw the folk and walk up the road like a deep sea diver, with lumps o dried mud fallin oaf in ma wake. A take ma buits oaf at the back door an bang thum thigither, tae git the rest o the muck oaf.

Ma opens the door. "Oh, it's you, son. How did yi git oan? Did yi manage awright?"

"Ay, A managed fine, ma. Here's the twa pound fur yi."

"Yir tea's nearly ready, son."

"That's great, Ma, an A've got a bag o tatties fur yi."

"The tatties an the money'll come in very handy son."

"A think A'll jist hae ma tea, git washed, then go tae bed, Ma. A'm a wee bit tired, an A'll hiv tae be up early in the mornin.

Brian Inch

Millennium Thoughts

"What's it gonna cost?" This century,
death, despair, famine and pain,
never mind the price, enjoy the day.
Yom Kippur, Doomsday or All Fools –
drink a toast to the past –
to Auschwitz, the Dodo and Hiroshima,
to forgotten friends,
Ghengis, Josef and Adolf and Almighty God.
Here's to the new,
to famine, earthquake and war,
to the living and the dead!
Does this include Uncle Fred,
left his bones in Flanders' field,

or cousin Jeremy, never said much, except "Ta",
left scattered somewhere in Armagh.
The clock ticks around.
People gather about the steeple
to raise a jolly toast
for all those living and soon to be dead
before we stagger off –
pissed as newts
and ready for bed.

Star of Night

Star so white, star of night
shine bright upon the bairns
so small and full of fight,
before the kirk on the green
where cattle low in lament
and tinkers trail their wares
upon the market stages,
as furnaces blossom and burn
and the carnage rages,
amongst carronade and broadside
striding in fiery fume.

Let peace flush war away
down soapy streets where dying men
colour all before,
as tall chimneys rise and belch out,
riches and pensions of gold
among a population growing ever old,
where the young cry out in pain
as the world changes,
never to be the same
along those ghostly long walls
where old Antonine stood.

Marjory Halton

Enduring Melody

Occasionally the music hurts
Catches me unawares
A sharp thrust of bittersweet pain
Opens a wound so nearly closed

The recklessness of youth
Knows nothing of regret
A life not lived long enough
To guess what the future holds

Sometimes the music finds me
Steals in uninvited
So much buried, so much perished
Still touches chords of another time

Relentlessly the years increase
Oceans vast divide and separate
In this endless realm of space
Does the music ever find you?

Never Forget

His footsteps sank deep in the rain-soaked earth
Stones dug sharp into weary feet,
The searing wind tore through his clothes
as onwards he plunged by sheer will power

It was the strength of his mind that held him
fast to that violent war torn zone
where to linger or dream was a dangerous game
which could lead to the grave long before his time

An end of ideas, all hopes and ambitions
which seemed so bright a year ago
A newly-wed with so much to strive for
but here and now just pain and fear

How could he tell her what it was like?
His letters protective concealed the truth
She would worry still more, never sleep at night
If she knew what he knew on these foreign shores

He plunged on and on upwards and down
He stumbled and fell and rose again
Could that be his friend alone on the hill?
A youth of 18, now a man struck down

Autumn's Travesty

The regal deer
Majestic in the glen
Elegant creatures, erect and proud
The essence of serenity

The terrified deer
Alert to hidden danger
Swift to react with pounding hearts
to the deadly adversary

The harshness of men
Who choose to eliminate
For reasons acceptable only to them
Bring terror to the innocents

These lonely hills
Their refuge and their nourishment
Are transformed into alien ground
Their princely territory ravaged.

Barbara Hammond

Swansong

I haven't done anything wrong! All right I am only a word proc-essor not a blasted computer. I never pretended to be anything more sophisticated. She knew I wasn't on the forefront of tech-nology when she bought me. I was however easy to use, cheap and a good many steps up from that horrible little portable type-writer she had when I arrived. I was all she wanted. Well, that was what she said then.

For ten years I did everything she asked. I wrote hundreds of letters, dozens of stories. I even banged out her notorious novel. What thanks do I get? He went out and bought an all-singing-and-dancing computer. Access to the Internet, fax machine, a mid-Atlantic voice saying 'fill me up with paper and change my ink cartridge' – posing beetroot!

Suddenly there I am stuck in a corner and the letters and sto-ries are all being churned out by someone else, Well, good luck to the pair of them. They deserve one another. Who wants any more boring, mis-spelt missives anyway?

All right, all right, I'm not totally pig headed. I know my drives are getting worn, I take ages to warm up and my monitor has a tendency to go blank at unpredictable intervals. Still she isn't getting any younger either. It was the last straw when she printed out all my best work and stuck it in that understudy-for-a-television – especially the entries for the competition.

You traitor, that was mine. It ought to have been submitted in my print. I should have the honour of presenting work that was created on me. My typeface is perfectly acceptable; you've won prizes with me before. Those four pieces were not bad, in fact about the best I've done, even if I do say so myself.

Tomorrow is the closing date for submitting the entries. They have to be printed tonight or she's disqualified. What is that tin-pot little printer doing? It's gone all temperamental, that's what. It splodges ink, jams its paper, makes peculiar noises, every-thing except flipping print. Serves her jolly well right.

So now who's in favour again? I give serious consideration to going down myself. Still she did have me refurbished, even though she obviously thought I was second best. Those stories are mine. If I don't print them now no one will ever see them. Knowing her, she'll have even better ones for next year. Go on you can have them, but I'm not happy.

The poncy computer is better now, but it's not so full of itself either, having let her down at the vital moment. It's especially disgruntled as the first prize certificate is hanging on my wall. She calls me 'Old Faithful'.

Put that in your ink cartridge and print it whiz kid!

George Hainey

Ode to a Road

They've long since done away with the mule
but the road is blocked tae Tomintoul

They teach the kids great stuff at school
but the road is blocked tae Tomintoul

They've got space ships with expensive fuel
but the road is blocked tae Tomintoul

They get television from Istanbul
but the road is blocked tae Tomintoul

They've got computers and the slide rule
but the road is blocked tae Tomintoul

They can send a delegation to Kabul
but the road is blocked tae Tomintoul

If you go up north remember you'll
find the road blocked tae Tomintoul

If I'd my way they'd be on the broo
for the road is blocked tae Cockbridge too

Liz Hawkins

Picture This

A cold dreich day in mid winter. How to entertain a small child was uppermost in my mind, so I put on a video – hailed as the modern substitute for nannies. We snuggle up on the couch, a wee girl of two and Grandma, and off we go into Wonderland with Alice.

Lewis Carroll's immortal literary classic comes to life in the hands of the Walt Disney studio: the white rabbit frantically running through the story, late for a very important date, with Alice in hot pursuit, always being held up by all the characters she meets on her journey. The Cheshire Cat's confusing directions, the March Hare and the manic Mad Hatter who invites her to a silly tea party; then there's Tweedledum and Tweedledee and their tale of the curious oysters, featuring the Walrus and the Carpenter; and we end at the palace of the Queen of Hearts and her enchanting playing cards, where anyone who angers the Queen gets their head chopped off. Lucky for Alice she wakes up in time, but not before she has found out where the white rabbit was going in such a hurry.

Walt Disney produced this film in 1950, but as long ago as 1922 he had the idea to make a combination live – action – animated film. The one he had his heart set on was *Alice in Wonderland*. Unfortunately, Laugh-O-Grams, the company backing the production, collapsed into insolvency and Disney was left with little to show for his efforts beyond the bitterness he felt having to leave a half-finished film and thousands of dollars in unpaid bills.

In search of new projects, he became interested in sound cartoons, and with Patrick Powers, who had a superior sound system to anyone else, began working on *Steamboat Willie* during the first months of 1928, in Power's New York studio. They incorporated the old vaudeville tune 'Steamboat Bill' and the familiar folk tune 'Turkey in the Straw' with the characters' movements, and added various soundtrack effects and, finally, the high-pitched squeaking voice of Mickey Mouse which Walt supplied himself.

On November 18th that same year *Steamboat Willie* opened at the Colony Theatre as a curtain raiser for the feature film *Gang War*. From its first scene featuring a whistling Mickey Mouse. It was obvious *Steamboat Willie* was what the audience had come to see. Thrilled and enchanted by the little mouse with the funny voice, they enthusiastically cheered his performance.

The surprising success of *Steamboat Willie* turned into a spectacular coup for Disney. He overnight became the hot new talent in the film industry. This was a stunning achievement for the twenty-six-year-old independent animator with no major studio affiliation or distributor.

As it would always seem with Walt Disney, his timing proved perfect. For if ever an industry needed a new hero, the movies did at that time. With Hollywood plagued by accusations of immorality, accompanied by growing threats of censorship, and about to be plunged along with the rest of the nation into severe economic decline, both *Steamboat Willie* and its maker arrived, as film heroes always seem to, 'just in the nick of time'.

Even as Mickey Mouse was becoming every kid's newest favourite cartoon character, his 'creator', the all-American hayseed from Kansas City with a fondness for farm animals who acted like humans, was about to become the least likely saviour of an industry filled with people – most of whom, in Walt's opinion, behaved like animals.

Whiz Kids

Where have all the snowmen gone
and all the laughing faces,
carrots for noses, buttons for eyes
sporting top hats and braces.

All along the streets
on all the garden lawns,
once snowmen proudly stood
with the architects looking on.

Where are the children
they must be around,
not one can be found.

No-one rolling snow or sledging
no-one hiding behind walls,
waiting for a victim
of their flying snowballs.

Flying through the air and bursting
giggles and children running,
it was such a tonic, they must be around –
yes, they have been found.

Eyes glued to a screen engrossed,
a whole generation
playing on computers.

Whiz kids with much too sharp a wit
pressing fingers on controls,
making figures jump through hoops
and parents feel like nincompoops.

Scenes of fun in the snow
the glowing faces and hillside races,
sledges with runners gleaming
children screaming. Are few now.

Elizabeth Ferguson

Turn off the Chicken, Darling

Turn off the chicken, Darling,
I won't be home for tea.
It seems I could be hours yet
So, don't wait up for me.

Nose to tail, row by row,
Side by side for miles.
Three feet forward hand brake on.
It's going to take a while.

Stranded cars with bonnets open,
lorries out of water.
Crowded cows in wooden crates,
heading for Gibraltar.

There's a 'silver slinky roller',
two along but one.
The drivers rather 'dishy' too.
I think I'll hang around.

His hair is dark; with streaks of grey,
his shoulders fine and broad.
His neck is thick, his ears just right,
His nose and lips look great.

Oh no! he's caught me looking,
he's winking in his mirror.
I'll pretend to read my book,
and ignore him altogether.

Good grief, he's coming towards me,
he's gorgeous, I was right.
Darling, turn off the chicken.
I won't be home to-night!

I Fell in Love with a Knight One Day

I fell in love with a knight one day

'Day' did I say?
I meant knight.
In shining armour he rode into my life,
made me free.

'Free' did I say?
I meant captive.
He captured my heart, soul and mind.

'Mind' did I say?
Yes, I did mind.
He loved me, vowed he would never leave me.

'Never leave me' did I say?
I meant he left me.
Widowed and broken, bewildered and sad.

'Sad' did I say?
No, I meant happy.
Happy to have know him, his kindness, his love.

'Love' did I say?
Yes, love,
Everlasting, unchanging, undying, forever.

I fell in love with a knight one day.

Catherine McArdle

Evening Encounter

It was almost dusk, but the sun was reluctant to sink and was splaying out long, blood-red fingers into the sky. The stone walls of the Palace were mellow in the fading sun, but shadows were gathering in the corners and the shape of the fountain in the courtyard was merging into the wall behind.

The custodian jangled his keys impatiently. "Look Kate," he said, a bit curtly, "it's only a cat. It'll find a corner to curl up in. It'll be OK."

I hesitated while he shifted from foot to foot. It was only a cat – a beautiful, black cat with enormous amber eyes that had looked at me, only me, all day. We had found it in the morning sitting on the cobbles by the fountain, looking proudly aloof yet forlorn. On seeing me it had run forward with a pleased little noise, half purr, half miaow, and curled itself around my legs. It had allowed no-one else near but stayed close to me all day. Now, just as I had been about to take it home it had disappeared.

The clinking keys interrupted my thoughts and I said quickly, "You go home, Bill. I'll have one last look around for the cat and then lock up."

Anxiously he peered at me. "You're sure? OK then, here's the torch. You'll need it. The sun's almost gone." And off he went through the massive stone archway, the wooden door thudding behind him.

Grasping the torch, I stood still, wondering where to begin my search. The Palace had many chambers and crannies where a cat could hide. As I set off to climb the winding staircase of the nearest turret, I shivered. Suddenly the stone which had been warm in the sunshine was cold and clammy. However I wasn't afraid. I knew the Palace well, and although there was an atmosphere of bygone days, it was not evil or frightening.

Stumbling a little on the worn, uneven steps, I remembered the tale of a guide who also stayed late in the ruins and had reputedly caught a glimpse of the ghost of James the Fourth. I would like to see him too, I thought, glancing behind me into the shadows. Making my way onward and calling softly for the cat, I stopped to peer through one of the slits in the battlements.

I could see the loch beneath, gleaming, quiet and still. Swans were making their way silently to nests under the trees by the loch edge. Branches made a tracery of leaves against the water. At the other side of the loch, tree trunks and twigs were etched black on the darkening sky. Standing there I thought of what life must have been like in the sixteenth and seventeenth centuries, with all the bustle of court life going on. What feasting, what revelry there must have been. Especially when James the Fifth had brought his French wife, Mary of Guise, to this very Palace of Linlithgow. What dancing there would have been in the cobbled courtyard, around a fountain flowing with blood-red wine.

By this time I had reached the Great Hall. I caught my breath for I had never seen the chamber in the dusk of evening. The hooded fireplace still dominated the area and I could imagine tables laden with food, stretching the length of the massive room. The walls would have been hung with rich, heavy tapestries, and, in the last rays of light, I thought I could see – not stone – but colours of soft gold and green. A small *miaow* pierced the silence and I saw the black cat sitting in a nook by the fireplace, as if that was its own special place. I moved towards it, speaking gently, but it suddenly looked from me, past me, into the shadows.

Slowly I turned. Eyes widening, I stared. Fear squeezed my insides. Every cliché I had ever read about fear and had always scorned proved to be true. My scalp did prickle, as if unseen fingers were stroking my hair. My breathing seemed almost to have stopped. I felt faint and my surroundings whirled as did the apparition in front of me. However amazement began to banish fright for the figure was a girl. And the girl who stood there could have been me. Her hair was dark, long and softly waved like mine, although lightly covered by what was a mixture of a snood and a nun's veil. Almond shaped, deep-blue eyes were arched over by smooth, dark eyebrows. Her cheek bones were set high in an oval face and sensitive lips were beginning to curve into a gentle smile. She was a mirror image of me, save for her clothes. For she wore a long, flowing robe in a colour I had never seen, some shade between lichen green and yellow gold. Her bodice, cut low and square, was edged with dark green embroidery, as were her full sleeves.

As I gazed, mesmerised, the cat reached her side, and, bending low she picked it up, hugging it close to her. She smiled again and I whispered to her urgently, "Your name? – What's your name?" Her lips framed the word as the cat looked back at me with its amber eyes. But they were both fading, blending into the shadows on the stone. Was it her voice or the sigh of a breeze that said *Kate*.

I sat for a long time in the corner where the cat had been. Numbly, I retraced my steps, crossed the dark courtyard, glancing unseeing at the emblems of another age on the fountain. The entrance gate swung into place with a bang, shattering the silence, although I could hear shouts and laughter from some youngsters spilling out from the light and warmth of a local pub.

I turned and looked at the Palace. It stood against the sky like a black, three dimensional picture. The loch beneath shone silver. I wondered if, in those past centuries, Kate had danced in the courtyard. Perhaps she had danced on the cobbles to the music of lute and lyre, even on the very day when the fountain had gushed forth the rich red wine of France. I would never know. I would go home to my own black cat. My black cat and I would keep our secret.

Adders in Glen Vorlich

We saw the adders, black,
zig-zagged in electric yellow-green.
They slept in coiled contortions
under hot sun.

Heaps of poison, they
slumbered on crumbled stone
of crofts where man once lived
long ages past.

Opening evil eyes, darting
forked tongues in silent hatred,
they slithered into jungle
of long-stemmed grass.

And Ben Vorlich, long-shouldered,
proud and ageless as time,
looked down on discarded skins
curling like dried leaves.

Looked down, through its stream-edged, grassy glen,
at tiny figures as we turned to climb again.

Poison

Where cliffs rise like carved rock temples,
where sea waves crash and shatter
into foaming spume,
where fields stretch into
forever's flat infinity
– they built Dounreay.

Then words unknown before, crept into
the lilting language of wild Caithness.
Uranium, potassium,
plutonium, nuclear material
in in deep waste shafts,
– words of death.

They built towers and squares of grey concrete,
and hard balloons that will never fly
but stand outlined
against barbed wire
and grey-blue sky, and
– signs of danger.

When they leave will they tear it down,
or will it stand crumbling, decaying
until it dies
and buries itself,
a concrete grave
– in deep earth?

It will disappear and be forgotten
but in the beauty of wild Caithness
death will still lurk.
It will lie under green cornfields
exist beneath waves
in murmuring sea.

And rocks will have poison in their veins.

James McDonald

The Implausible Dream

Welcome to 24 Hour World News, coming to you from the Vorderman Dome. Where, before setting out on his post work experience, our Illustrious Leader, Mr Bill Hague, is giving his retiral 'Address to the Nations'.

I am just hearing that Mr Hague has started his address, so we are going live into the Vorderman Dome to hear Mr Hague.

. . . and the heavens above it. He put in the sun and stars, he gave us the fish and the whale. He gave us every living creature that walks, crawls and creeps upon the earth.

Then He created man, giving him dominion over all these things, all of the things he had created in six days. On the seventh he rested, leaving man to carry on his work.

If He *had* worked the seventh day, how much easier our lives could have been. Many years of back-breaking toil would have been saved, had he given us the wheel. Cold nights spent shivering in caves would have been much more bearable, had he given us fire with the means to control it. All these hate filled wars would have been avoided, had he given us *euthanasia*.

Through euthanasia we have eradicated our world of all hereditary disease. We have given our world citizens a standard of living once only enjoyed by royal households. With our population controls we have made sure that each and every one of us is never hungry or ever idle.

Retirement now holds no fears, knowing, at the age of thirty-five, we have a full five years to enjoy the latter days of our lives in a style befitting our seniority. And on our chosen day, when our time comes for processing, our final hours could not be happier, the virtual reality machines in the twilight centres allowing us to relive our dearest and most precious moments.

In this, my final speech before I retire to enjoy my post-work years, it is my duty to address the nations and answer the critics of our regime. On this day, the fiftieth anniversary of Martin Luther King's Sermon on the Mount, I can say to each and every one of you, 'The dream has arrived'.

Fifty years ago, Martin Luther King addressed one nation, a nation deeply divided by racial hatred. A nation whose Declaration of Independence was a rubber cheque which bounced on black people. Today, anyone bearing that cheque will be paid in full, no matter the colour of their skin, or the choice of their religion. Today, I address the world community, in the certain knowledge that all men are created equal.

Today, not only do the sons of slaves and slave-owners sit at the same table of brotherhood, but they walk hand in hand through life, sharing their dreams and aspirations during two score years. And on their chosen day, as they walk over the hill to the twilight centres, these dreams and aspirations are passed to their children knowing that, on the threshold of adulthood, they too can look forward to enjoying a full life, during the remainder of their years.

"Two score years is not enough!" I hear critics say. "Give us early retirement! Give us ten post-work years." Here is my answer to these critics.

In 50 years we have transformed not only the state of Mississippi into an oasis of freedom and justice, but also the battle grounds of Europe, the killing fields of Asia, and the Arid Deserts of Iraq and Iran. Would you have us turn from this oasis? An oasis that King could only dream about? Would you have us turn back to a land that swelters in the heat of oppression and injustice?

Martin Luther King had a dream. A dream that black boys and girls could walk hand in hand with white boys and girls, as brothers and sisters.

Today, from the age of ten, our young black and white citizens share the learning screens in our Universities. At 15, with their education complete, they spend the next five years in the procreation camps singing and praying together in a symphony of brotherhood and love.

Today, I say to Martin Luther King: we have the realisation of your dream. Euthanasia has given us the means to control the lives of our citizens, without the conflicts of the past and the prejudices of your time.

Today, I can say to Martin Luther King; the bell of freedom is ringing, not only in the Rockies, but in the Himalayas. Ringing not only from Stone Mountain, but from Table Mountain. Not only from the Alleghenies, but from Kilimanjaro. From the hilltops in New Hampshire to the rugged mountain peaks of the Cuillin, the bell of freedom is ringing loud and clear.

Today, as our most senior citizens walk the glorious road over the hill to the twilight centres, Martin Luther King, they are singing, "Free at last. Free at last. Thank God Almighty we are free at last."

That was our illustrious leader, Bill Hague, addressing the nations live from the Vorderman Dome.

News just breaking: it has been reported that the two aged rebels, Donald Dewar and Alex Salmond, have been sighted with a seditious faction of the Tartan Army in North Britain. Their capture is expected soon.

Kevin McKenzie.

Just One More Fag

It was the fifth day of my latest non-smoking campaign. I had tried to stop several times before with varying degrees of failure. The temptation to try just one cigarette had always proved to be too strong for me.

I had been advised by some of my ex-smokers friends to keep a few cigarettes in the house to combat the feeling of predestined or pre-determined misery, but, sitting at the fireside, my eyes were constantly drawn to the packet of cigarettes on the mantel shelf.

To distract my attention from the noxious weed, I took a few chocolate biscuits from the packet and started to nibble them. Ben, my Labrador dog, came towards me with that 'I want one too' look on his face. He had been trained not to take a biscuit until told to do so, so when I put one on the coffee table he just sat down patiently and stared at it. Thin streams of saliva running down his chin in anticipation.

Throughout the evening I avoided the temptation for 'just one cigarette' and decided it would help if I went to bed early.

I slept fitfully and awoke the following morning irritable, miserable and desperate for a fag. Finally, deciding that enough was enough I grabbed a cigarette from the bedside table. With trembling hands I flicked the lighter into life and lit up.

With a sigh of relief I sat on the bed and felt the welcome effect of the tobacco flow into my nicotine-starved body – I felt good.

I walked into the living room and saw the chocolate biscuit lying on the coffee table. Sitting beside it was Ben – patiently waiting.

I realised the temptations that this dog had overcome, but he had remained true to the obedience that he had been taught. I felt weak, spineless and ashamed of myself. This dog – the dumb animal, had a far stronger will than I would ever have.

How could I ever again honestly say that I was his master?

June Gardner McKenzie

The Girl from 'Red River Valley'

Dear Falkirk Writers.

Howdy! Ah'm writin to you good folks at the writers' circle, because, Ah guess, you are ma last hope. Ye'see, Ah ain't had no writin as such or book learnin. You will see by the postmark Ah'm now settled in Tombstone, Arizona, where Ah was born. What's left o ma kin folk still stay hereabouts.

Ah would die a happy woman if Ah could settle a few things in ma mind.

Now, Ah'm tryin to locate an old boyfriend a mine, name a Frankie Falkirk. Leastways, that was one handle he was known by 65 years ago. The other was 'fast draw' Frankie. Frankie's kin folk came from Falkirk, Scotland, an Ah hope you good folks will be able to find him.

Ah spend most o ma time now just a-sittin an a-rockin on ma back porch re-callin ma memories o Frankie.

Ma mind is crystal clear, an seein this is the year o the millennium Ah've been doin some memory-searchin, cos, one thing's for sure, Ah ain't never gonna see another.

In the old days Frankie wrote me a song. You writin folks might know it – 'Red River Valley'. Then, Ah was kinda hankerin to leave the valley, but Frankie pleaded with me, in the song, not to leave. Bright eyes, he said, (he never called me by ma real name) bright eyes, he whispered, you an me belong together.

Well, folks, between his soft voice an guitar strummin, what was a lone country gal to do? We sat on the rocks overlooking the valley an he sprouted poetry, an told me sweet stories he had wrote. He was good at the writin – that's why Ah was a-thinkin, if he had high-tailed it back to Falkirk, Scotland, he might hitch hissel up to your writers' circle.

That day on the rocks Frankie gave me a locket an inside it was a picture of the steeple. Bright eyes, he said, one day Ah'm gonna take you to see ma kin folk in Falkirk. He told me the bairns o Falkirk were known world-wide for their hospitality and honesty.

Ah guess he was excluding hissel a mite because a week later Frankie high-tailed it out o the valley with Rosie O'Grady, the saloon keeper, and the contents o the First National Bank. It was then, folks, that Ah kinda re-gretted ma decision to stay.

The Sheriff of Red River Valley, then, was big Elmer Kincaid.

A real hard-ridin, gun-totin hombre who always got his man, an he was hell-bent on a-catchin Frankie.

Big Elmer formed posse after posse an scoured the territory, daily, but failed to find Frankie. Bein a determined crittur he then turned his attention to Frankie's old buddy an pardner, Mohican Mick.

Now, Mohican Mick's pappy was a one-eyed Irishman named Kelly an his mama, Passin Cloud, was the daughter o a Mohican chief. Some folks still maintain Passin Cloud didn't pass through the valley quick enough.

Sheriff Kincaid could not pin a single thing on Mick and this drove him wild. He took to his bed, a broken man. As he lay a-dyin he handed his badge and gun to his son, Clarence. Now, young Clarence was a mere shadda o his old pappy. He had a sorta 'delicate' nature, an was known to the boys in town as Kinky Kincaid.

Kinky soon lost control of the town's rangy varmints. They formed a lynch mob an strung up Mohican Mick in Dead Man's Gulch. A United States Marshal arrived, pronto, to restore law an order. His name was Marshal Ward. He restored law an order so well he was able to run a small mail order business on the side.

But that's enough o ma re-callin, folks.

Now, some friends o mine have been on vacation to Scotland. They took a lotta pictures o your home town, Falkirk, an ah was especially interested in two o them. One was a photo o the steeple an the other of a saloon called 'Rosie O'Grady'. Naturally, Ah've been a-won'drin, is this a coincidence?

If you good folks knows anythin about Frankie's whereabouts, Ah sure would be mighty glad to hear from ya.

Mr Silas P Moneypenney the 3rd, the bank manager in these here parts, came a-callin. Tell them good folks in Falkirk, he said, that the bounty on Frankie has been upped to 5,000 dollars. Dead or alive. It's a lotta dough, folks, an Ah would be pleased to split it 50-50 with ya.

Now folks, Ah reckon Ah would like you writers to know ma real name as Frankie never mentioned it in the song.

Ma best wishes an ma thanks to you all.

Esmeralda K Finklestein.

David Russell McLean

Tactical Woo

Why do we fumble a practised review
Pressure one of our senses be first in the queue
Then as ardent emotions stir, each wholly subdue
Could fate be daured?
Would fate respond tae a tactical woo
Tae strike yon cord

Will she smile, our cue observe
Speak wi her usual feminine verve
Accept we probably could unnerve
Wi glaiket patter
We must pursue wi honest nerve
Or face the latter!

'The Closed Shop'

(multiple rejection)

You as faction have your way
As I compelled tae sorrow
While each may grin their smile away
This pen will steal tomorrow.

Ma hert you've sunk in consequence
As I sae pleased wi diction
While aa concerned in jubilance
Yer guid points are but fiction.

Denied me once, denied me twice
Denied me three times, blatant
Of aa the folk brought up on vice
It's you wha hauds the patent!!

Two Limericks

A delinquent wee dug, his domain
Maist pavements an parks would aye stain,
But when chasing some sheep
It didnae come cheap,
'Cause yon fermar approved a heidstane!

A marauding wee mouse fae Milngavie
Inadvertently slept a long lie,
He was caught in the pudding
And that's no including
Infringing some rules of Versailles!

Pat McLaughlin

A Millennium Thought

O how extraordinary life would be
If our planet Earth from hatred could be free
No violence no ethnic cleansing in our world
With flags of everlasting peace unfurled

Love and thoughtful caring in each heart
Before the new millennium makes a start
Without God's love our poor souls are lost
Like a ship in a storm battered and tossed

If only people would see the light
They would be freed of their miserable plight
Helping each other to bear the pain
The world would be a much better place again

How amazing the rich nations seem to me
Can find destructive, devastating, arms when need be
At a few hours notice anywhere they like
But seem so slow when a real disaster strikes

Hours and days seem to pass by
While thousands of poor souls drown or die
Before a real decisive move is made
However it takes time to arrange such aid

Kate Mulvey

The Way We Live Now

Strangers offering me gifts or favours always arouse my suspicions. I learned very early that there's no such thing as a free lunch, and, sadly, experience has confirmed that there are no exceptions to prove this rule. I'm never tempted by the plethora of special offers from grab-now-pay-later to free holiday flights which fills so much space in newspapers and magazines. I usually pass smartly on to the interesting bits, but a programme I saw on television recently set me thinking. It exposed the hidden agenda, and has given shopping a whole new dimension for me.

Those so-benevolent loyalty cards pressed upon us at every checkout in supermarkets are far from innocent. When acquiring one we are asked for various details of personal information, all quite straightforward, nothing too probing, not unreasonable when credit is involved. Anyway most of it is available from other sources such as the phone book or the voters roll. So we get onto another such register, and naturally once we have this helpful painless easy-to-use storecard we can't wait to try it out. We find reasons not to shop in any of the other stores. We are hooked.

This is where the game begins. From the information we've supplied much more about us can be deduced. Sales slips are analysed and preferences noted leading to targeting with special offers we just can't resist. When and where we shop is charted from our till receipts, more opportunities for the hard sell.

Now that the small square screen Rules OK vast amounts of data are processed at the flick of a mouse. Customers are categorised. Singles go for gourmet meals for one; bottled water; couples buy prepared foods and exotic sauces for assembly cookery; families fill the trolley with assorted breakfast cereals, 3 litre bottles of fizzy drinks, plastic packs of raw meat and vegetables for some real cooking. The elderly shop economically for small amounts, traditional foods, loose tea. The marketing people make good use of these details.

When the store has you conditioned, concern for your comfort and convenience is not a priority. At first you may not notice how much stamina is needed for this kind of shopping. You have to get there, which will take longer than a stroll down the High Street and will almost certainly require wheeled transport, your own or public. Once among the aisles you will walk miles to assemble the items you want. Should you fancy something from the specialist counters, cheese or cooked meats for instance, you will have to take a numbered ticket and wait till your number comes up. But you need not stand in line, you can stroll around and indulge in impulse buying from displays strategically placed to encourage it. The extra cost will not worry you, not at the time. Your flexible friend will take care of it, for now.

When you get to the checkout you will join a long queue waiting to file through, a bit like a sheep dip or the fleecing shed. You may even decide to pay with your new Switch card which will have the money out of your account before you get the goods home. You will hoist each and every purchase onto one end of the rolling track and off the other. In fact each goody will be lifted (probably by you) at least five times before it reaches the cupboard or the fridge. Count them. I never understand why mothers with small children go to exercise classes. If you add to this scenario unloading and reloading a brace of toddlers from and back into a car, and a push-chair, a young mum nowadays has to be fitter than a professional footballer.

The management cuts down on overheads by getting the customers to do work that once provided full-time long term jobs. Workers are needed only to keep the shelves filled up and to take the money. Not a lot of job satisfaction in that. But they are always adding new developments.

In many of the bigger stores you can have a scanner of your own which will record and add up your purchases as you go and present you with the bill at the end. This should cut out a couple of the weightlifting workouts, but trials have shown up a few teething problems, like goods not scanned, inadvertently of course. It seems the ordinary punter will be required to pass a training course, and will only be trusted with the scanner after passing a test in its use. I kid you not.

Supermarkets defend themselves by telling us this is what we want, though they aren't very convincing about how they know this. They say this gives us a better lifestyle. Better than what and for whom? It's always worth asking. They say they can assess our tastes, get to know our preferences, offer us treats. They claim they save us money. They don't tell us if they've included the cost of transport, time, energy and temper – ours. They don't mention that, of course, you have to have enough money in the first place to be able to buy the big economy size and take advantage of special offers.

Some of us remember the way it used to be. You gave your friendly neighbourhood grocer a shopping list once a week. At the weekend a boy appeared on the doorstep with a box con-

taining your order, all correct and neatly and securely packed by
expert hands, no squashed loaves or bashed biscuits. He carried
it in and put it on the kitchen table. You gave him sixpence. He
was pleased, and so were you, and you had the things put away
in no time, less than you spend now just getting to your nearest
store.

It's designed to separate us from our hard-earned tax-paid
cash. Like lemmings, the unwary rush to join in.

Doreen McCulloch

A Wee Swim?

M   Millie decided to go for a swim naked in the sea.

I   Isobel had other ideas and bathed naked.

L   Lily decided to join Millie as it was so hot.

L   Larry waded in with his trouser legs rolled up.

E   Ethel was mortified at the nakedness, and went in fully clothed.

N   Norman was excited at the sight of Millie, but decided his fat belly was a turn off, so declined.

N   Norman was excited at the sight of Millie, and decided his fat belly was a turn on, so jumped right in.

I   Iris the book worm buried her head in her book.

U   Ursula swanned about in her long flowing organza dress with her stone-studded tiara on her head, puffing at her fag through her cigarette holder. No way was she getting wet.

M   Morris was the gentleman of the group dressed in his white suit and bright red dotted cravat. He was bemused by the whole scenario, drank everyone's leftovers of champagne, soon to fall down into a stupor.

Edna K Morrison

Poco Moco

Every town has its sights. Along with parks, statues, civic build-ings and historic monuments I would include those local char-acters whose features or eccentricity of behaviour set them apart from their fellow citizens. They may be comic or tragic fig-ures but they are always destined to be outsiders.

Some fifty years ago, in Stirling, we had Poco Moco. Although no one knew how he had acquired the name it was the only one by which we knew him. By day he roamed the streets of the town, favouring the older part around the castle, the Church of the Holy Rude and, to the great delight of its pupils, of whom I was one, the area around the High School.

There were rumours that he had been a soldier, some said an officer, discharged because of his addiction to alcohol. This might have been true, as Poco Moco was indiscriminate in his intake, relishing whatever his few coppers could buy, be it beer, cheap wine or even meths.

Because of this and the fact that he had no fixed abode he dossed down in closes and doorways for the most part with the occasional night in the 'model' lodging or the police cells depend-ing upon how enraged he was when awakened by his unwilling hosts.

His face was bloated and weather-beaten, rheumy eyes squinted out beneath bushy eyebrows, a straggling 'Paw Broon' moustache concealed the mouth while the area in between was dominated by a large bulbous strawberry-pitted nose.

This last feature was celebrated in Poco Moco folklore. It was said that when the Good Lord was allocating earthly features to the souls in heaven waiting to be born he had at one stage called out 'Noses' and Poco Moco, whose ear allocation must have been slightly sub-standard, thought that he was handing out roses, called out "I'll have a large red one, please", and God obliged.

His clothes were shabby and redolent of years of living rough. Boots, baggy trousers, shirt, stained jacket, with the addition of an old raincoat in winter, were on occasion graced by a once-white muffler and the whole ensemble topped by a battered 'bunnet' or trilby. In one hand he carried a stick and slung over his shoulder was a hessian sack which contained the few pos-sessions he had accumulated as he lurched through life.

We youngsters had many a brush with Poco Moco. The more

daring boys would call out after him as he passed, but made sure before they did so that they had a clear getaway as the violence of his reaction depended on his degree of sobriety. Although on occasion we tormented him we did feel a certain affection for him as his unpredictable behaviour and lack of respect for our elders, or even the Law, made life more amusing.

As we sat in maths class labouring over some fiendish problem we would hear him singing as he patrolled his territory. Or, even better, his ripe earthy language would assault our ears as in the street below he verbally abused some innocent passer-by who had gazed on him too critically or too long.

By the late fifties I had left school, married and was living in Grangemouth. It was May and Stirling was in the throes of its first Arts Festival so after work we decided to visit the Smith Institute where an exhibition of Dutch paintings was on show. To our surprise we seemed to be the only people apart from attendants in the building and it was not until we entered the second room that we saw another visitor.

There standing in front of a Rembrandt self-portrait was Poco Moco, slightly greyer and more bent with the passing of the years but Poco Moco nonetheless, stick in hand, sack at feet with a bunch of wild flowers tucked in his hatband – his usual sartorial concession to spring and summer.

Eventually we joined him in front of the picture. It had been painted in the period when Rembrandt was rejected by a society that no longer considered him 'fashionable'. His beloved wife Saskia had died, as had three of their children, and he had been declared bankrupt. His eyes mirrored pain, confusion and a sense of hopelessness. I wondered what the old tramp thought when confronted with this man, whose face mirrored his, feature by feature.

After a few minutes he recognised our presence. "That's a great picture," he said to us. "A great picture by a great painter." Then he picked up his sack and marched out into the soft spring evening.

Ever since then whenever I see a Rembrandt self portrait I think of Poco Moco and wonder what became of him.

It would be sad to think that he ended his days huddled in a chair in Stirling's 'Poor House', gazing out over its high grey stone wall topped by shards of broken glass. But for me he lives on in my memory, singing and swaggering around the old town in his flower-bedecked hat.

G S Mutch

The Queen Mother

A better poem than John Betjeman's
Should not be too hard
Although I am not the Poet Laureate
Simply the Larbert Bard
As we speak about her with one another
Don't we think she is just like our dear mother
A wee Scots lass doing the highland fling
She captured the heart of a future King
As reigning monarchs during World War Two
They faced the bombs just like me and you
When her husband died and she was all alone
Her spirit and character the world was shown
Elizabeth her daughter is now our Queen
The likeness to her mother is there to be seen
Pride in her grandson Charles is well known
Longing for the day he ascends the throne
A birthday present to exceed all others
One which she would share with all grandmothers
May we wish you a happy birthday and be so bold
I will write again when you are 100 years old.

A Poem for the Year 2000

When I last wrote a poem for the Queen Mother
I said twenty years on I would write another
as this is happening on the millennium year
it will be an occasion for everyone to cheer

Let's hope at last she will see the world at peace
and all the bombing and killing will cease
Britain could give the lead in this crusade
saying no more arms for export will be made

The United Nations can make a start
by showing they will play their part
forming an army to help keep the peace
then the world may see all wars cease

This you may think only a pipe dream
but not as difficult as it would seem
if only we could stop all the greed
and be satisfied with just what we need.

Russell Ogilvy

It's Reigning Cats

The letterbox on my front door rattled urgently. This surprised me a little bit as the box cover was placed on the very lowest part of the mainly glass-fronted entrance, and was usually only used when the postman delivered my morning mail. I reluctantly put down my cup of breakfast coffee and opened the door. Winston, from next door, slouched through the entrance, shoulders hunched up tight. He shambled into the front lounge and wearily lay down on my capacious sofa, raised his right arm and pointed through the window at the car slowly drawing out from our avenue.

"Those two buggers have done it again," he sobbed. "They have deserted me once more." He cried, and tears ran down his ruddy cheeks. "Not a drop of bloody food or drink have they left, while they run off to enjoy themselves."

He wiped his damp cheeks piteously, and whimpered quietly, "I can only throw myself on your mercy, and ask you to save me from dying of hunger and thirst. Please show me a little kindness and I will be forever in your debt."

I should perhaps now give a little clarification to this heartbreaking scenario, and explain that Winston is my neighbour's ginger tomcat, and that I had seen him devour a large heap of expensive cat food just an hour earlier that morning.

I had been expecting Winston to call in sometime that day, although not just quite so early. He put on this 'deserted bride' act every time Bill and Mary Smithers from next door went off on a holiday, even although he knew that adequate supplies for him had been handed in by his domesticated and well trained owners.

Further explanation is also needed to clarify my remarks about a talking cat. You may think my imagination is running away, but, although Winston was a cat, he and I had developed a form of communication from the first time we met. I am from a highland family, and have the inbred ability of all highlanders to read, or feel, what goes on in the minds of animals. This is not a psychic ability but more of a developed sense, similar to that held by shepherds with their dogs, lion tamers with their lions, and as shown in recent Hollywood films, horse whisperers with their horses.

However, enough of that and let us return to my cat tale.

Some seven or eight years previously Bill Smithers had shown me a little ginger ball he was holding in his opened fist, "This is Winston, our new cat," he said. I, myself, am not a 'cat' person, but I poked the bundle and muttered, "He'll be dead within a week." The little ball unfurled slightly, opened one eye, looked up at me and quietly said. "If you poke me like that again I'll bite your fucking finger off."

I didn't let on to Bill that he had a foul-mouthed feline in his care. His wife was very sedate, and I was sure that the first mouthful from the small bundle of sunshine would get him a quick shove out the front door, with no cheery goodbyes; but he was fortunate, she adored the soft cuddly little bundle and was not able to understand what the piteous little mewings really meant. To put it more succinctly, for wee Winston there was no catastrophe.

A further example of this ability of ours to communicate is shown in the following instance. One cold day Winston rattled the letterbox in his usual imperious way, and when admitted, ran up the stairs to his favourite spot by the large central heating radiator. I give him a shout, telling him that I had just bought some smoked mackerel from the fishmonger that morning. He stopped his mad scamper as he reached the top of the stairs, turned round, came back down, ran into the kitchen and stationed himself in front of the fridge. He and I both enjoyed the smoked mackerel.

This, however, was a bad move on my part. The fishmonger came in his large van every Thursday morning, and so, every Thursday morning after the van moved off, my letterbox rattled and a ravenous streak of red lightning shot into the kitchen, imperiously looking up at the fridge until I meekly served my rightful lord and master.

You may think from this mournful tale, that the neighbours Tom and Mary were not the best of animal lovers, but this is definitely not the case. Winston wined and dined on the best of fare, he slept in a luxurious cat box in the warmest part of the house, and if he ever felt lonely, he just popped into the Smithers's bed for company. The fault with Winston was that he was from a long line of stage door cats who had had been based at the Alhambra theatre in Glasgow, thus explaining his abuse of the English language. He also had the feeling, given to all of the acting fraternity, that he was superior to all the lower, non-acting classes; to which most of us in this small town belong. He put on this show for all the neighbours in the district, who treated him with due respect required, feeding and succouring him in response to his acts of tragedy and doom.

As a further example of my own capability to communicate with animals. I cite the following. My daughter has for many years been married to Angelo, a well-known magician and illusionist and they live and work on the island of Majorca. They own, or perhaps I would be better saying, they live with a large menagerie of animals, including two very large and fearsome tigers that appear to consist solely of gigantic teeth and razor sharp claws. They have a tiger's ginger colouring and both have a family resemblance to Winston the stage-struck tomcat. There is now a new addition. a very young white tiger that rolls about the house like a playful kitten, although with very sharp claws. The other animals roam about in complete harmony with everyone, and I know that my daughter has my gift of 'talking to the animals', although she, herself, doesn't realise it. I see her passing the time of day with the dogs, and they all seem, without being told, to know what she wants them to do.

This last paragraph is a form of grovelling apology to real cat lovers, putting me in my proper place, as it were. The finale of the spectacular show takes place with my daughter disappearing from a locked cage and being replaced by Saba, one of the ferocious tigers. Angelo then enters the cage, pets the tiger, puts his head in the tiger's jaws and is rewarded by having his face licked. The tiger appears to be a fierce beast straight from the jungle, but in fact is quite tame with his master. Saba, the tiger, does not speak to me, and I put this down to the fact that he has lived in Spain all his life, and that my knowledge of Spanish is very limited. Although he does not speak to me, I wonder why it is that every time he sees me he licks his lips . . .

Excuse me, I must go. My letterbox is rattling.

Janet Paisley

Sculpting

The knife knows what it deals with:
earth, wood or stone. It allows
what it feels to guide the stroke,

always freeing. Blood would run
on this blade were it flesh carved
but this is wood, a knotted root.

The form shakes loose of constraint:
spilled soil, flaked bark, rotted stick
and in the centre what holds good;

man and woman entwined, shaped
underground, by dark, by growth.
I do not pretend to know

what forces make the forests,
nor why stones wait for finding.
Hands see what heart will not admit:

his back is strong, her limbs lithe,
inextricably they writhe
the brutal agonies of love.

Happens

"Hingy."
"Hingy?"
"Ay. Hingummyjig. Ye ken?"
"Naw."
"Ay, ye dae. Hingmy wi the big . . . em . . ."
"Chist."
"See you, jist cause you've nane. Him, ken."
"Heid then."
"Dinnae be stupit."
"Weel whit?"
"The big thingmy."
"Motor? Hoose?"
"Och, whitje caw it?"

"Whit?"

"Dug. The big dug."

"He husnae got a dug."

"Naw, bit ye ken wha ah mean."

"Ay. Run ower, win't it? When wis that again?"

"A while noo. Ten year?"

"Nae wey."

"No be faur oot. Oor Magrit seen it, mind? Comin hame fae school."

"Ah mind that. The state she wis in. Howlin hur heid aff."

"That's whey they pit the crossin in."

"Wis that then?"

"Coorse it wis. An she's bin workin six."

"Git awa. Jees, ye ken ye're gittin oan a bit. Oor Tam wis thirty last week. Thirty. Ah telt him he'd an awfy cheek."

"Ay. Well, same time he wis in a stushy aboot that wean."

"It wisnae his."

"We aw ken. Oneybody's that yin. An the laddie MacFarlane's spit whin she wis born."

"Aw comes oot in the waash, ken."

"Bonny lassie, bit. Nice wee thing."

"Must be aboot ten, right enough."

"See?"

"Crossin fur a dug, eh?"

"Ay. It wis a mess, bit. Magine if it hudda been a wean."

"Aw, wheesht."

"Happens."

"Awthing does. So whit aboot him then?"

"Wha?"

"Thingmy."

Andrew Peacock

Mega Bucks Mega Blunders

When the oil boom was at its height I went to work for Megabucks Oil, one of the World's biggest oil production companies. I was taken to my new office then introduced to my colleagues in the department, all of whom seemed exceptionally friendly, joking and laughing as they were introduced.

Next I was taken to meet the various people with whom I would have to collaborate, again impressed by the friendly and informal attitude which I'd discovered prevailed in the whole building. When lunch time came my mentor had to excuse himself and leave me to my own devices. Knowing Aberdeen quite well by this time, I adjourned to a nearby pub which I knew served meals. After the congenial welcome it felt a bit strange be to sitting on my own, when who should walk in but two of the guys I'd been introduced to earlier. They collected their lunch from the bar and, without hesitation, came across to join me.

The conversation started in the usual way with the normal enquiries about my previous employers, their scope of work, attitude to staff, future prospects etc etc. But they were obviously keen to continue the animated conversation they'd been having as they came in the door and continued while they waited at the bar to be served.

So I was then treated to one of the most amazing conversations I've ever heard in my life. Here is the story it told.

All oil platforms create their own electrical power to operate, heating, lighting, cooking, instruments etc, using Aero Engines, burning the ever-present excess gas from the drilling process. Most of the gas at that time was 'burnt off' using the flare stack, but this was stopped as being far too wasteful of a scarce natural resource.

"How has the situation arisen?"

"It was quite simple really, Bill was asked to find out which Platform Aero Engines required a new conversion kit, to enable them to burn the gas coming from our oil fields at that time. He was supposed to check which engines required this kit by looking through the appropriate drawings and files."

"And he didn't do that?"

"Well, yes and no. He was a bit busy and it was quite a time-consuming job, so he checked three or four at random, found that they were all exactly the same, so, to save himself the time and trouble, he simply ordered one kit for each engine."

"And they weren't exactly the same?"

"No way. Six of the engines were of a newer design which doesn't require the modifications."

"So how long did Bill keep his job?"

"He's still got it. Until someone queries why there so much room in the stores is wasted because of those six big crates, lifts the tarpaulins off, and checks what's inside them."

"When might that be?"

"Well, they've been there for months already. They've even been moved once or twice, because they were in the way."

"Oh my God, and just how much has this mistake cost?"

"In total so far, and not counting the continuing cost of storage, over *three million pounds*."

Val Pöhler

Singing High High High

Miss Wilkinson was bored. Bored with dusting day after day, with counting the pennies, even with the gardening. She missed the man next door who had tended to her small patch for thirty years until he died and the house was taken over by a young couple who seemed to have dozens of screeching children.

One day, she studied her bank statement then counted the money in her purse. Yes, she could manage it. She was going shopping but this time not for food. She was going to buy something for herself. She dug out her red felt hat, the one with the flowers on the band, and steamed it. After choosing an outfit with care – old but still smart, she thought – she stuffed an umbrella into her shopper. She wouldn't want her good hat spoiled by the rain, if it did rain – you could never tell nowadays, the climate was so temperamental.

The store was busy and, for a while, Miss Wilkinson did nothing but wander. There were so many nice things, she didn't know what to choose. Finally she halted in front of a fashion display. The skirt was unusual, in a colour they called harvest although she would have said mustard.

She cleared her throat. "Excuse me, Miss." The sales girl continued a fascinating conversation with her friend.

Miss Wilkinson spoke a little louder. "Excuse me, I'd like to see that skirt." The girl flipped a corner of the skirt. "This one, you mean? It's the latest in linen," she said indifferently.

"Yes, I think I'd like to buy that one – if you have it in my size, that is."

She became rather flustered by the sales girl's rather superior attitude and ended up carrying home not one, but two skirts. One termed harvest, the other, porridge. A daft name, she thought, for such a delicate shade of beige.

The next day, dressed in her new mustard skirt, she went for a walk in the Botanic Gardens. It was a warm sunny day and after a while she began to feel peculiar . . . lightheaded and . . . light-hearted. She felt as if she could fly, soar high above the clouds and speak to the sun. Giggling, Miss Wilkinson looked at her feet. They were firmly planted on the ground. She giggled again. Fancy saying her feet were planted and here she was in the greenhouse. She started to laugh.

"Do you mind if I ask what the joke is?" The voice from behind her was warm and deep. She turned round to meet the man's gaze. His smile was as warm as his voice and the silver slivers in his hair caught the sun's rays.

Miss Wilkinson, without a further thought, launched into an involved story. It ended with both of them laughing helplessly as she amazed herself with her flights of fancy. The man introduced himself. "Martin Boyd – and you?" He held out his hand.

"Dora Wilkinson." She took his hand, feeling an unaccustomed tugging at her heart. "It's 'Miss'," she added quickly, feeling somehow it was important for him to know that.

"Miss Wilkinson," Martin repeated formally, then his eyes twinkled, "or should I say 'Miss Dora', or even 'Dora Miss'. I think I'll call you 'Dormouse'." They started to laugh again and she was glad to accept Martin's invitation to go to the patisserie for a coffee. They parted with his words ringing in her ears. "I'll call for you tomorrow afternoon, if that's all right with you."

It certainly was all right with her. She could hardly believe what had happened and she hardly dared think of what was going to happen the very next day. She was reading the local paper that evening when some words leapt out at her.

'Clothes from Cannabis' was the headline above an article describing the latest linen-type fabric which came in shades of smoke, porridge and harvest. Dora felt her stomach knot as she read on "derived from Cannabis Hemp, the much disparaged and maligned Marijuana plant . . ." Porridge! And Harvest! She ran upstairs and looked at the labels on her new skirts. Yes, there it was. Sinking onto the bed, she read the paper again. So that's what had been wrong with her yesterday, thought Dora. She must have been high!

Cheeks burning at the thought of what Martin would say when he found out, she read, "There's no 'high' from hemp fibre". Little did they know!

Back in her armchair, she went over the previous day's events again and again, catching thoughts and worrying at them like a puppy. Should she tell Martin? Did he really have to know? After all, where was she likely to meet another man as nice as him, at her age too! By bedtime she still hadn't made up her mind.

The morning sun striped her bedroom wall as Dora awoke and stretched. She blushed as yesterday poked its head into her sleepy brain. Still undecided about whether to say anything to Martin about the skirts, she showered then opened her wardrobe door. As if her hand had a mind of its own, it reached in for her new skirt, the porridge one. Ah well, she sighed, I suppose that's what you call fate. What was wrong with porridge for breakfast anyway.

They went to the Art Galleries that afternoon, finding a shared love of Impressionism. By the end of the day, they had found a common bond in many things, particularly humour. She learned that Martin was a widower and from then on, their rapport grew into something more than friendship. Dora felt completely transformed. No more mousy Miss Wilkinson, no more felt hats. She wasn't sure whether it was because of Martin or the skirts, which she wore day after day. She only knew that she felt wonderful.

They often went for drives, to the hills or the coast, sometimes accompanied by one of Martin's two daughters. It was just the two of them walking along a seaside promenade when Martin proposed. Dora stopped, her heart doing some peculiar flips.

"But . . . but . . ." she stammered, "two old fogies like us . . . what would everyone think? Your family . . ."

"No-one will be the least bit bothered. You're the best thing that's happened to me in years and I think we should make the most of it and get married." Martin's eyes held a glow as he looked down at Dora and added, "Besides, it's been ten years since Betty died and I think the family will be happy for me to remarry. You like them, don't you?"

"Oh yes, very much."

"And they like you, so what's to worry about? That's settled then. We'll make it soon." Dora loved it when Martin was being masterful and for while they behaved like love-struck teenagers.

His daughters were delighted to hear their news and enjoyed helping Dora with all the planning involved. As she had no family, she was particularly pleased when Martin asked his brother Roy to give her away. His other brother, Tom, was to be the best man.

Dora felt like a young girl as she walked up the aisle on Roy's arm. After the honeymoon, in their new home, they were blissfully happy. The only bone of contention was her clothes. She wore the two skirts so often that Martin eventually was forced to comment. "Why do you keep wearing these all the time? You know you can have anything you want. I enjoy buying you things."

"I feel good in my skirts," was her reply. "Don't you want me to feel good?"

Martin couldn't argue with that one but there came a day when he put his foot down and insisted that the skirts be consigned to the dustbin. Dora felt a shiver of apprehension tickle her stomach. She *thought* her nature had changed but she was unsure. Too unsure to ever think of doing away with skirts that still gave her a buzz when she wore them. she pushed them into the back of the wardrobe but kept snipping scraps from them to pin inside whatever outfit she was wearing.

Then she caught the flu, a severe bout. Martin nursed her for a fortnight, until Dora tottered out of bed one morning, determined to get dressed and go out. She opened the wardrobe, pulled out some clothes then rummaged at the bottom for one of her magical skirts. She rummaged . . . and rummaged . . . but no pieces of anything were to be found.

"What are you looking for?" asked Martin as he came into the bedroom with a breakfast tray.

"Oh, er, just some old pieces of cloth I going to make into dusters some day."

"That reminds me, Mrs Parker asked for some donations for the church jumble sale, so I went through our wardrobes and gave her a few things. And remember those old skirts of yours? They were buried under a pile of stuff – it looked as though the moths had been at them so I threw them in the dustbin."

She stared at him in consternation. "But I wanted them," she stammered. "I . . . I . . . was going to use them again."

As Martin looked at her thoughtfully, Dora turned away and caught sight of herself in the mirror. She looked again. Was that Miss Wilkinson making an appearance? She shivered, wondering if Martin would like Miss Wilkinson.

Who Said That?

When I consider how my life is spent, ere half my days
the time has come, I staunchly said, to write of many things;

yet what a tangled web we weave when first we practise to devise
but be it hard to find a theme, I vow I'll never plagiarise.

A verse! A verse! My kingdom for a verse!
Was this the foot that launched a thousand ships?
On with the scan! Let joy be unconfined.
If winter comes, can spring be far behind?

If anything might rouse me now the kind old sun will know.
I shot an idea in the air. It fell to earth, I knew not where.
Possibly it went to seed under the spreading chestnut tree.
No inspiration here, but plagiarism? Not for me!

I must go down to the seas again
my thoughts as idle as a painted ship upon a painted ocean.
So I will arise now and go to Innisfree
when the blue wave rolls nightly on deep Galilee.

Drowsily hot, I sat on a train that stopped at Adlestrop
when all at once I saw a crowd, a host of golden daffodils.
Fair daffodils I weep to see you haste away so soon
but I won't plagiarise on you – I'll try out a lampoon.

To rhyme, or not to rhyme, that is the question;
the best laid schemes of June and moon gang aft agley
but I rush in where Angels fear to tread.
No plagiarism here, if I can keep my head.

Poems, poems, burning bright in the forest of the night
but do not go gentle into that good night
as the curfew tolls the knell of parting day
for words seen by candlelight may not look the same by day.

Twas brillig and the slithy toves did gyre and gimble in the wabe.
Is this a poem which I see before me, the title toward my hand?
Where did you come from, ditty dear? Out of the everywhere into
   here.
Hail to thee, blithe jingle! I give plagiarism a sneer.

When I am dead, I hope it may be said
Her sins were scarlet but her poems were read.
Hope springs eternal in the human breast –
no need to plagiarise, I'm at my best!

Isobel Quinn

Bear

Waking from his long winter sleep, bear meandered down into the valley towards the coastal areas in search of new plant shoots. A couple of weeks later he ambled up the hillside in search of ants, bird eggs and the first of the berries. As spring moved into summer, bear migrated towards the river for the spawning salmon. Here he found a spot below a waterfall where the fish were plentiful and the other bears scattered further down the river left him alone, intent on their own fishing.

After eating his fill of fish, bear headed back up the hillside looking for mushrooms, nuts and berries. Foraging for food, he unearthed a bees nest and, despite the angry bees, enjoyed the sweet sticky honeycomb inside.

Now full of honey and other delicacies, he found a safe place behind a large flat rock and settled down for a nap. Stretching in the sun, bear was aware of distant sounds.

Somewhere in the recess of his mind he could dimly recall loud bangs, the searing pain in his shoulder and his mate slumping to the ground, the baying dogs surrounding her and the shouts of the hunters. Bear's wound had healed but he still had a scar where the bullet grazed his shoulder. Instinctively, he headed for the safety of the trees and managed to keep one step ahead of the hunters and their dogs.

As the leaves began to turn brown, red and gold bear returned to the mountain and passed his days by using his long claws to dig up squirrels, marmots and mice to supplement his diet.

Now he sniffed the air. Having eaten well, his grizzled fur was thick and heavy. Lumbering up the hillside, his paws pushing aside the foliage, he found the hidden cave and crawled inside. Lying down on a bed of pine needles, bear closed his eyes as the first snowflake fell.

Martin Richmond

Screw the Job

The prisoner of today refers to the officer pounding the prison gallery or chained to his wrist at court as a 'screw', much as he has done throughout the penal system for many years in the United Kingdom, USA, and Canada. Other more colourful descriptions are used as well but 'screw' is the most common and most accepted terminology, at least by the criminal fraternity, but very few could say why or where it came from?

In 1853 the third Inspector for Prisons in Scotland, a Captain John Kincaid, introduced to Scottish jails the 'crank machine'. It was not an instrument of torture, although some might term it as such, but a device to provide intensive labour, not only to the long term prisoner on hard labour but also to the short term prisoner as a form of punishment. The machine stood approximately 4 feet high as a circular, metal drum on four legs with a crank handle projecting from its side. Three of these machines were purchased for Scottish jails at the princely sum of £5.10s and set to work.

One of these machines was placed in the Argyll jail of Inverary, where its inmates found if they committed any infringement of the rules, or a misdemeanour against good order and discipline, what it had in store for them. An inmate's normal employment within the jail would have been to make and repair nets for local fishermen and pick oakum to make ropes.

Inverary jail was a local jail, which meant that those living in its vicinity, who had committed a crime and were found guilty in its courthouse which was conveniently situated alongside the jail, would carry out their sentence of up to 9 months there. If their crimes were more serious and they received a stiffer sentence they would be transferred to Perth prison.

Some crimes incurred the sentence of transportation and the 'guilty parties' would be transferred down to an English port for onward delivery by sailing ship to Freemantle in Western Australia. The practice of transportation ceased in Scotland with the last ship leaving in 1867 carrying an ex-postmaster who defrauded the post office of £200. In today's terms this would be equivalent to £30,000.

Possibly an example of trying to *stamp* out crime by *posting the* criminal down-under, first *class?*

Returning to the subject of the crank machine, its introduction to Scottish jails as a form of punishment was recommended by the Prisons board based in Edinburgh after a somewhat successful run in its place of origin, Pentonville Prison in London, around 1840. There they used it as an alternative to breaking rocks in local quarries, or sometimes a prelude to this to 'break them in' to it.

In the jail at Inverary, which is now an award winning living museum, the machine was placed in the cell of the prisoner who had broken the rules and as part of his punishment he would be required to turn the crank handle a specific number of times per day. A counter on the machine confirmed this target and if it was an adult male prisoner he would be required to register 14,400 revolutions per day. A female prisoner would have to achieve 9,600 turns and a young male offender 12,000. The English male prisoner in Pentonville would only be required to achieve 10,000 revolutions, which could suggest that the Scot was made of much sterner stuff, or the Scottish 'screw' much meaner?

Whilst the prisoner toiled at these turns the considerate warder, who thought that not enough effort was being applied to the task, would turn a screw on the rear of the machine increasing the pressure of weight required to turn the handle. Hence the term 'screw' was applied to the warder and has stuck ever since.

So the next time you come across a prison officer, whether on a social or professional level, you could inform him or her that they owe their nickname to a 19th century machine, and to the third Inspector for Prisons in Scotland, Captain Kincaid.

Most modern prisons are equipped with 'state of the art' exercise machines nowadays and the prisoner chooses to use a machine that exerts pressure on their muscles to build strength, keep fit, or simply pass time. The prison officers also use these same machines to exercise on and you could say that it's now 'the turn of the screw'?

Information on Inverary Prison obtained through curator Mr Jeff Parks with thanks.

FRUITFULFILLING

Seeking sweet, citrus solace,
From the conference chairman of the pears,
Is the clinging peach of fruitless endeavours?
And the fanfare for fruitful affairs.
Picking plum parts for pomegranates to portray
Forces tidal red currants to ebb and flow,
Then seductively, they juicily peel away.
The lime and reason of rhubarbary grapes
Reveals raspberry blowers are repentant.
While the pineapple ring cares not a fig
For each darling clementine lost forever,
To damsons in distress but independent.
Ultimately the presidential apple crumbles,
Pipped at his post he cannot be reached,
Although this top banana is ripe for the picking,
By taking the pith he will be impeached!

Hitch – Concoction
(a movie tribute to Alfred Hitchcock)

The lady vanishes behind the torn curtain
just a paradigm case of stage fright
She left in a spellbound frenzy,
down thirty nine steps in the night.

Blackmail was, without a shadow of a doubt,
the cause of Rebecca's vertigo.
I confess suspicion of her secret past
once being a notorious psycho.

She took up with entirely the wrong man,
a man who knew too much.
The trouble with Harry was taxidermy,
stuffing birds and such.

They met as strangers on a train,
on the North by Northwest line.
The fat bald man in the corner
had been there all the time.

John Sneddon

I am the Stumbling Block

I have the power I have the will
with a vengeance to cause havoc
I contain evil have no remorse
I am the Tibfem

Clards I'm the Tibfem
The alien force
I play the knave hah yeah

Clards who have you
Klasrads
I play the knave hah yeah

I am the stumbling block
I am the stumbling block
I am the stumbling block
I am the stumbling

Clards expect no sympathy
of my divbell symphony
I play the knave hah yeah

Clards I stoke the fire
you will retire
I play the knave hah yeah

I am the stumbling block
I will annihilate the rock
I am the stumbling block
I am I am

I will blow you away
into mystic disarray
and oblivion is imminent yah

I have no compassion or conscience
and I am irrational
I have no porve wah

I'm the forked tail
will put you off the rail
the mardonicly rule
for they are slaves of Tibfen

I am the stumbling block
I am the stumbling block
I am the stumbling block
I am I am yah

Do not beg
do not beg
Cuts no ice
I will consider
your fate
electrecute or burn
Do not beg

I am the Tibfen

Idols

An idol is adoringly defined
An image used as an object of worship
To be blunt a false god
Do they suffer from repercussions.

Or do they have no conscience
And deliberately misguide
Others take a page out of their book
And follow like lost sheep.

They hold an important role
And are the modern pied piper
Not all are negligent
But, let's face it, is the majority?

They are copied wholeheartedly
Sometimes the consequences can be costly
I am certainly no preacher
Friends let's be sensible.

If you commit an offence
It could be repeated
This is no way to learn civilisation
And I do admit some are harmless.

But remember this
Would they take your grave
Indeed I say they will not
Please do not intimidate the blind.

Dorothy Whamond

Into the Millennium

It was at night, coming down the hill from Slamannan, that a bursting, blinding explosion of lights first appeared across the darkness, lights that moved and twinkled, while against the sky-line tall chimneys spouted living flames. Beyond were the dim outlines of ships lying at anchor. In the early days it wasn't called Grangemouth. When the first lock was built it was Sealock. Some years later, when the SS Wawaloam and the SS Rotterdam lay in the harbour, it was known as Little Holland; that was when there were as many Dutch seamen as Scottish walking the dockside and the Queen's Pub in South Bridge Street served schnapps. The present name is taken from the slow-flowing Grange Burn which passes Grange School, Grange Church, and flows down to Ronaldshay Crescent.

In the 18th century Grangemouth imported more Scandinavian timber than any town in Scotland, and by the end of the 19th century this was its most profitable industry; many sawmills were established for the manufacture of railway sleepers, telegraph poles and pit-props. Today the road into Grangemouth runs past vast timber-yards with high-stacked bales, wire-bound and resin-fresh. These timber basins were well-known for the great flocks of swans which nested there. But there are no swans today.

There was a whale, however. As late as the 1950s a lone whale swam up the Forth and Clyde Canal to the entrance, where, eluding attempts at capture, it died and had to be 'flenshed' on the spot.

The whaling ships had come into Grangemouth from the early 18th century. In the 1960s traces of the original whaling trade were discovered: 'Whale Fish Company' was painted on a wall underneath North Basin Street. There was also the remains of a whaling vessel and a 'Whale Boiling House' for the boiling of blabber. This had been closed down in the early days of the town's growth – there is, understandably, reference to objections raised against 'noxious trades'. But this was the forerunner of the oil production which was to become Grangemouth's most powerful industry, leading to the giant oil refinery and the production of petroleum.

Prosperity from oil and allied chemical industries provided impetus for the building industry and local amenities for the fast-growing town. The Earl of Zetland build Zetland Park, well-known for its tree-lined walks and fountains, but most of all for the widely-criticised war memorial which depicted the British Lion savaging the German Eagle.

Even during the General Strike of 1926 a Queen was crowned there on the annual Children's Day, when the little girls were resplendent in white frocks and straw boaters, the boys in Sunday suits and school caps, all flying the coloured ribbons of their schools. In the background, the name 'Rigregazzi's', above a shop front, showed the popularity of Italian ice-cream. Summer galas were held at the Grange Burn, where later an outdoor pool was built, with changing rooms and spectator balcony.

Another feature of early photographs were the 'drag horses' used for pulling vessels along the canal. When traffic on the canal was discontinued the big stable-yard on Station Road was closed down, being demolished in 1954. The horse troughs were removed from the streets and the fire engine no longer went out with a clatter of hoofs. And the whole town felt relief when the shameful 'hitching rail' was removed; for years it had been a heart-rending sight as knacker horses were tied there in rows, head to tail, every Friday night, to stand without food or water until Sunday morning when they were loaded onto a ship bound for Germany and the sausage market.

It was 1803 – long before the more famous Comet, that the little steamship 'Charlotte Dundas' took her maiden voyage along the canal, towing two loaded vessels each weighing 70 tons. The town's pride in the 'Charlotte Dundas' was demonstrated by including her in the coat of arms; she sails there beside the stag's head which bears the horns of the Cross on its antlers. Underneath is the town's motto: *Ingenium Vincit Omnium*.

The age of the engine had arrived. Soon the saw-mills were mechanised, then the first taxi appeared on the streets. Produced by Fitzcharles, this was a high, small-bonnetted vehicle with convertible roof and white-walled tyres. Some years later Fitzcharles brought out the first bus, neat, white and streamlined, which became very popular for excursions. The days of the gigs, the dog-carts, the high-piled delivery carts and the carriages of the gentry were numbered.

1939 saw the opening of Grangemouth Airport, HQ of the Air Training Corps, and later the Gliding School. The stately mansions of the oil magnates were turned into hotels; the villas in the High Street, having already surrendered their railings and iron gates to the War effort, were converted to offices, with car parks where their gardens used to grow. British Petroleum had become the town's largest employer, as the sole producer of petrol in Scotland. Closer and still closer on the sky-line were packed the cooling tanks and towering factories.

From Slamannan hill at night the town seems to be spreading further and further across the dark sky, a sheer bright energy horizoned by tall ships, black towers, and fiery chimneys. It is a picture of light, of power, of a reaching out towards the years to come; at the same time it recalls the stag's head, the Cross and the steamship, and the calm confidence of the motto that leads Grangemouth into the Millennium: Ingenuity Conquers All.

The Listening Face

"I have my listening face," she said,
"and when I'm bored at parties
or poetry readings, I put it on."
It comes complete, the steady gaze
fixed on the speaker, eyebrows raised
in faint surprise, amused delight
at a cliché or pathetic pun:
eyes drop, contemplative, at lines
quite senseless, or that just don't scan.
I have a smile, a tapping foot
for the dull galloping anapaest,
and when I gaze entranced, I'm trying
to count the pages still to come.

He laughed. "But do you . . . ?" he began.
His voice trailed off. He stopped.

Her eyes were fixed on him,
steady, contemplative.
The tapping foot . . . oh surely not!
Was this, in front of him,
the listening face?

82

Fifteen Minutes in Carthage

The hotel bus pulled up at the shore.
"Just fifteen minutes," – the courier's voice.
"There's nothing much to see." Not much.
Just grey curved sands where loud waves crashed
relentless on the evening shore,
tall pillars and white crumbling walls,
a headless statue. Near the rocks
an old woman tended a fire
of driftwood and dropped paper scraps.

Carthage. Through thin dusk shadows moved
as round us the noise of armour rang,
and helmets flashed in bright noon light,
while sails billowed to meet the breeze
where the long ship waited in the bay.
Here, from the sea's edge, Dido called
in vain, dark robes like a pall
behind her, as Aeneas sailed,
cruel in his splendour at the prow,
nor turned nor looked shoreward again.

The fire died out and fine ash blew,
acrid and death-like, on our cheeks,
sharp image of her funeral pyre –
the flames fierce on the darkening sky
the smoke, and salt taste of her tears.

The bus was waiting as we left
the shore, where now the long tide rolled
gently on empty sands grown dark.
Just fifteen minutes. We moved away,
long headlights cutting through the night.

Sheena Burnett White

Memories of the Women's Land Army During the 1939-1945 War

In 1942, when my country informed me it was in need of man-power, the local labour exchange gave me the choice of working in munitions, the dockyard, as a process worker with ICI, a rail-way porter in the goods station, or in The Women's Land Army.

I chose the latter, which seemed the least of all the evils. I was kitted out at the Stirling headquarters and sent to Lord Rose-bery's estate at Dalmeny, South Queensferry.

The uniform gave me a certain confidence, also a feeling of authority. Brown breeches, green V necked jumper, brimmed hat with badge, thick woollen knee-high socks and heavy brown lac-ing shoes. A muddy-brown coloured tie completed the outfit. Wearing my green jumper and breeches, I looked every inch the picture of the land girl I'd seen pinned to the wall of the Stirling HQ. My new-found confidence was short-lived.

Three other girls working on the estate wore shapeless khaki dungarees, which were also part of the clothing issue. Less glam-orous, but more serviceable. They wore scarves – tied like tur-bans – on their heads, not so much to protect them from dust and dirt, but to cover the leadtape curlers which seemed to be per-manent fixtures in their hair.

Harvest time. Field after field of corn. The tractor driving round relentlessly, cutting it down. It was gathered, tied into sheaves, and stooked in bundles of four. My bare arms were lacerated by the sharp ends of the corn stalks. At the end of the first day, I wished I'd taken the job of railway porter in the goods station.

The memory of my first instruction in the Land Army will remain with me for ever. Standing in a large cart, pulled by an even larger Clydesdale horse, it was necessary to catch the sheaves of corn pitchforked up by the farm hands and lay them in an orderly pile in the cart. The sheaves were coming up fast and furious, so I shoved them down anywhere. A man's voice shouted angrily. I looked down from the cart. A tall, scrawny man, in a bunnet, was glaring up at me.

I couldn't make out a word he was saying. "Pardon?" I said, politely. The shout came again. This time I did understand.

"Put them with their bloody arses oot." Which translated means stalk ends outwards – corn heads inwards.

Spreading coups of dung on large fields, over a long period of time, had a profound effect on me. I found myself declaiming Mark Anthony's speech over Caesar's dead body as I forked the coups of dung and spread it left, right and centre.

> 0, pardon me, thou bleeding piece of earth,
> That I am meek and gentle with these butchers!
> Thou art the ruins of the noblest man
> That ever lived in the tide of times!

Approaching the bottom of the field, I'd reached –

> That this foul deed shall smell above the earth
> With carrion men, groaning for burial.

An audience of six greeted me. Two ploughmen, three farm workers, and the grieve. The stony silence was broken by one of the farm hands. "It's that daft lassie frae Grangemouth." I moved from Dalmeny to Cambus, Clackmannanshire.

A large stone house requisitioned by the Land Army was used as a hostel. About sixteen girls were billeted there and we were moved around the various farms. A warden woke us up each morning about 6.30, and a cook provided us with a hearty breakfast before we left for work.

Milking a cow looks deceptively easy. All my cows seemed to have choked udders and the swishing tail would constantly whack me round my turban as I leaned against the side of the beast. The dairymen produced pails of frothy, creamy milk. My pail when it wasn't kicked over by the cow, was flat, hairy and only half full. It was obvious I would never make a dairymaid.

I have vivid memories of the first time I drove a tractor. It was a bright orange, high seated machine with huge, sweeping mudguards, called a Minneapolis Moline. Ploughing up and down fields, going through the same ritual with the cultivator or harrow hooked on, was, without doubt, the best part of the whole Land Army experience.

The reeds was a large indoor enclosure which housed the bullocks. Across the yard stood a barrel of black treacle which was used to lace their feed. It laced mine also. I held many a slice of bread under the tap of that barrel. Spread with treacle and folded over, it made a brilliant sandwich – satisfying and very, very healthy. On a cold winter's day sitting on the back of a resting bullock, I'd happily munch my 'piece'. Gathering straw from the ground, I'd push it into my boots for extra warmth. Between a cosy seat and cosy feet, I was in seventh heaven. The heat from the bullock was ten times better than any hot water bottle!

At the corner of the stack-yard was a single, covered stall with a door leading in to it. For some obscure reason the farm hands were trying to persuade a bullock through it.

The beast had other ideas, and spent its time dodging them.

They tried throwing a rope round its neck, and pulling it. The men pulled – the bullock pulled – and of course, the bullock won. The men went flat on their faces. Yes, an element of farce crept into the proceedings.

I was standing near the door of the stall, and, by a sheer fluke, the beast came towards me. I remembered a voice saying, you can hold a calf at the top of its tail and guide it – like a bike! Well, I thought, if it works for a calf, it may work for a bullock. I thrust out my arm, grabbed the top of its tail, and gave it a sharp twist. The bullock roared and leapt forward. My hand slipped to the dungy mass at the end of the tail, and still clutching it, we both disappeared into the stall.

In the dark interior, I truly expected to be kicked in all directions. A rusty iron ring was attached to the stone wall. I grabbed it, closed my eyes and waited for the worst. The bullock staggered round, missed me by inches, and charged out the door again.

Still clinging to the ring, I heard a voice. Looking over, I saw Bain, the farm manager, framed in the doorway. "Guid sakes Lassie, it's the bullock we're wantin in there, no you."

The arrival of the threshing machine triggered off great activity. Beans were dirty things to thresh, and by the end of the day I'd be covered in black dust. Round my turban I tied a gauze scarf – yashmak fashion. It was wound round my neck to protect me from the bean soot, which infiltrated my lungs.

From an Italian prisoner of war camp near the farm, two POW's were sent to help at the threshing. They wore brown battle dress tops with yellow circles on the back, and brown trousers. With help from a POW, my job was to collect the chaff spewed out from underneath the machine. It was dragged in an old bit of sacking and thrown into a barn.

By the end of the day we climbed a mountain of chaff to empty the final sacks. It was exhausting, depressing and dirty.

In a damp corner of Clackmannanshire, staring at a noisy threshing machine, two forlorn POW's looked as if they were wondering what it was all about. As was the land girl.

When the bottom of a stack was reached, rats, lurking there, would be trapped. Terriers were sent in to flush them out. They would attack the rats, which retaliated by biting the terriers on the nose, often drawing blood.

I was wearing knee-high gaiters, buckled over my dungarees. I remember, with horror, a huge rat came blindly at me and clamped itself on the front of my gaitered leg. One of the dogs went for it and the rat let go and fled, to my intense relief.

Sometimes, the workers, just for fun, would lift a dead rat by the tail and sling it between the bales as they clamped together. My revulsion at the sight of the squashed rat produced even more hilarity.

Early one morning, I went with the stockman to collect a truck load of bullocks from the station. He 'whooped' and whacked them with a stick, driving them towards the farm. Half way there, six bullocks broke away, making for a wide gate leading to a large mansion. The stockman shouted "Get them back". So, 'whooping' and waving my sticks I went after them.

The house had a crescent shaped drive with gate posts at either end. The wrought iron gates, which would have prevented us from trespassing, had been removed. All iron was requisitioned in wartime. We crashed past a wide bay window at the front of the house. I had a fleeting glimpse of the astonished faces of a family having breakfast, and a large packet of cornflakes.

With a few more ineffectual whacks, we swept down through the other gate, and rejoined the herd. Trying to control the bullocks was like trying to control the waves.

What the stockman said to me is unprintable.

Shortly after that 'cattle drive', I left the Women's Land Army. But we still won the war!

Tommy Thomson

Mary's Dumpling

Mary brocht it in, cut in little pieces,
Piled high it wis. That's lots, she thocht,
Wis that richt? Na! Na! Nay chance,
Cos, one got there afore them aa,
And of course it wis. 'Twas I.

While the others drank their nips,
Naebody noticed that a little feast had I.
It wis wi heavy heart, Ah passed the plate,
Jist so they say they had a bit or twa.

Wi loosened belt I took my leave,
My pouches bulging full,
Oh Mary, please, please jist fir me
Mak another twa or three,
Ay! Jist for me.